... Tony's personal, down-home, easy to understand methods and techniques will help both novice and expert — young and old alike. Any fisherman can gain decades of great smallmouth fishing experience between these pages .... and remember, female smallmouth bass are terrific kissers. God is great — life is good today.

—Jimmy Houston

Tony Bean has more passion and knowledge about "Smallmouth Bass" than any man I know. This book will make anyone a better angler.

— Denny Brauer, Professional Bass Fisherman

Tony Bean is an awesome smallmouth fisherman, and finally he's sharing his knowledge with everyone!"

— Shaw Grigsby, Professional Fisherman

The Last Smallmouth

Tony Bean
WITH DARREN SHELL

© 2010, Tony Bean
& Weuffer Daffer Productions LLC

All Rights Reserved

No parts of the book may be recreated in any form without the expressed written consent of: Tony Bean, Darren Shell, Weuffer Daffer Productions, and Fideli Publishing, Inc.

ISBN: 978-1-60414-272-3

Library of Congress Copyright Pending

Published by
Fideli Publishing, Inc.
www.FideliPublishing.com

For fishing tips, photographs and more fishing advice from Tony, visit:
www.SmallmouthSecrets.com

Printed in China

"I don't care what size my last fish will be ... I just want it to be a smallmouth."

~Tony Bean

This book is dedicated to my Father, Jim Bean, as everyone called him. While not a fisherman, he followed every cast I made and kept every article and picture of his son. My father spent his life training bird dogs and had many champions. It was his life. I miss him.

While I won't be able to share the pages of this book with my father, I look forward to sitting on the couch at Uncle Grady's and hearing the stories he so loves to tell. I will be able to tell him how important he was to the pages of this book and to me in my life. ~ **TB**

Contents

Forward .... *xiii*
A Note From Tony .... *xv*

CHAPTER ONE
Locating Big Smallmouth Bass 1
   Finding them is the hardest part 2
   Food Source at the House 5

CHAPTER TWO
Knocking on the Door of the House 9
   A Fun Story on *Feel* 20

CHAPTER THREE
Learning *Feel* 21

CHAPTER FOUR
Sales Pitch 27
   A fun story on documentation 35

CHAPTER FIVE
High/Low Barometric Pressure and Its Effects on Area of Influence 37

CHAPTER SIX
Baits—The Salesman's Product 41
   Grubs and Hair Jigs 43
   Swimming the Grub: 43
   Speed 44
   Control Depth 46
   Why did I learn this method and where can it help me? 48

CHAPTER SEVEN
A Short Note on Rods and Reels 55

CHAPTER EIGHT
Creeks Were Made to Wade 59
    The Presentation 66
    Baits 69

CHAPTER NINE
Colors 73
    A Quick Story 74
    Example 75
    Grub 78
    Tube 80
    Fly 80
    Another story on color 82

CHAPTER TEN
The Hair Fly 85
    Here comes another story 87
    Favorite colors 92
    Combinations: In either pork or fly applications. 92
    A Note from Darren on the Float-N-Fly 94

CHAPTER ELEVEN
Smallmouth Can Be Spoon-fed 97
    Let me share another little story 98

CHAPTER TWELVE
Keeping Records 105
    Another little story 109

CHAPTER THIRTEEN
Position and Presentation 113
   Zeroing in on the last.. 116

CHAPTER FOURTEEN
The Top-Water Grub... 123

CHAPTER FIFTEEN
Baits on the Bottom... 133
   Another story comes to mind … 136

CHAPTER SIXTEEN
Bouncing the Jig 139

CHAPTER SEVENTEEN
Nighttime Smallmouth Bass 145
   Time of night 146
   Another little story … I just love little stories. 149
   Baits at night. 150
   Nighttime top water. 151

CHAPTER EIGHTEEN
The Four P's of Fishing 157
   The Creek Fishing Experience 158
   Presentation. 162
   Proximity. 163
   Patience and Persistence... 163

CHAPTER NINETEEN
Smallmouth Through the Ages 165

CHAPTER TWENTY
Spinner Baits, Crank Baits, and Worms 171
   Crank baits, spinner baits and worms 172

CHAPTER TWENTY-ONE
Approaching a New Body of Water 175
   Approaching a New Body of Water 175
   Fishing the fictional lake. 177
   One Fish Does Not a Pattern Make 184

CHAPTER TWENTY-TWO
Flashers and Graphs 193

CHAPTER TWENTY-THREE
A Nearly-Forgotten Article 203
   The Great Smallmouth Hunt 203
   First find the pattern 203
   Testing The Theory 205
   Preliminary Strategies 206
   Asking Questions 209
   Early-Morning Efforts 210
   Afternoon Action 213
   Late Afternoon 215
   Quitting Time 216

CHAPTER TWENTY-THREE
"The Last Chapter" 221

Acknowledgements to fishing friends new and old 225
About the Author 227
About the Coauthor 229
Index 231

Forward

On a cold day in January, 2010, I sat quietly at my desk, typing away as usual. The windows of my marina were offering quite a show. Over one shoulder, the sparrows were toying in the snow, fighting over what the blue jays had tossed from the feeder. Over the other shoulder, a light blustery wind swirled over Dale Hollow Lake. My current computer work was boring me to tears, and my mind was thinking more about grabbing my float-&-fly rod and bundling up for a day on the lake. *I'll bet there's a smallmouth swimming right over there…*

Ring……

That dang phone shook me out of my fishing dream and back into reality.

"Hello," I mumbled.

"Mr. Shell?"

"Yeah."

"This is Tony Bean. You might not know me, but I've been a smallmouth guide my whole life."

I immediately looked up at my bookshelf. Sure enough, there was that tiny, blue, twenty-year-old book resting where it always did … when I wasn't pouring over it and wearing out its weathered cover. Even though I'd grown up on this smallmouth utopia of Dale Hollow, I still studied every written word about the subtleties of bass fishing. I'd also written a few books of my own about the history of this lake and its wonderful fishing. I'd made my living directly overtop of smallmouth heaven and had sucked up every bit of lake lore and fishing lore I could. I'd been from one end of that little blue book on my shelf to the other, studying all the smallmouth wizardry within and treating it like the "good book" it had become. The name on the spine read "Tony Bean".

So, like the professional writer and savvy businessman I am, I blurted, "Dude … I've got your book!!!!"

That's the day I first talked to the legendary smallmouth wizard, Tony Bean. My simplistic nature seemed to strike a cord with my new bronze-back expert buddy, and we immediately started making plans for his new book—the book he said would be his last. A lump swelled in my throat, hoping against hope that this man really had 50 more books left in him. *Last One?* Gosh, then he spoke the magic words…

"I think I'd like you to help me write this thing."

Holy Crap!

I have to admit. I love people. I love fishing. I love what I do in life—making my living on the water and typing out a few words that people can hopefully enjoy.

This book has been one more wonderful amendment to all the things I love. Thanks, Tony. Thanks for letting this old guy be the excited little kid to get that call.

~ Darren Shell

A Note from Tony

Most fishermen start fishing when the boat is sitting right where the anglers want to cast their lines. Not me. I start fishing (in my head) long before splashing waves touch my boat. Many, many things come into play when I think about my fishing trip. I plan ahead the night before, pouring over my maps and staging the next day's locations. I watch wildlife around me, especially on my way to the lake. If wildlife is moving, the fish will be too. It's one big life cycle and I take it in on my way to the lake. If the rabbits are darting across the road, dashing through my headlights, my favorite fish will be darting here and there, too. It's just the way the game is played. When animals are frisky and playful, fishing is usually playful for this old guide. ... And I like playing.

So, let's cut the fat and start talking real fishing techniques. Aside from all of Mother Nature's visuals, we can nail down mannerisms of smallmouth bass and use knowledge to help our hooks find home base. We can dissect the American Smallmouth Bass down to its bare bones and see what makes them tick … and see what will help us catch that elusive prey of golden muscle-man fish.

Common sense will get us there. We just have to break it down into simple, steadfast observations that catch fish. Tried and true methods will seldom fail.

Fisherman change, but fish only change with the stimuli given them. Yeah, they wise up to some fishing ways. The smallmouth isn't a dumb fish. It still acts on instinct. It still has Mother Nature pulsing in its veins. It still wants to bite something interesting in its usual boring path. But certain things like heavy line and particularly odd baits make the smallmouth wary. Pardon the pun, but they can smell something fishy…

So, my whole point of writing this book … perhaps my last one … is to capture the timeless ways of the Smallmouth Bass. We've made every effort to make sure nothing here is dated. Two decades from now—four decades from now, this book should still have something to offer the new bass fisherman. It should still have insightful ways to help people catch fish. That's what I want to leave for the world.

I've enjoyed many wonderful bass moments in my life. I hope I've captured them in book form for others. Little old me is wishing you, my reader, good fishing.

Tony Bean, oh … about eighty years ago or so. ☺

CHAPTER ONE

Locating Big Smallmouth Bass

Factors in Finding These Fish

Since childhood, the call of the wild has rooted itself within me right down into my bones. I feel its little sparkles like the warm sunshine on that cold winter's day when most would not dare to drag the ol' boat to the lake or cast into its frosty waters. When few will back their trailer down the ramp, I'll be the fisherman standing there bouncing like the little kid I once was, hoping and praying Uncle Grady would take me to the river or lake or farm pond. Nature has simply always played a part in my life. Me and Ma Nature go way back. She's always been my favorite fishing partner.

Let's take a moment to talk about nature. This is a bigger picture than you might think. Every fisherman should study his or her surroundings before loosening the old dock lines and untying the usual sailor's knot. Before that boat slides off the trailer, many things should be going through the smallmouth fisherman's mind. Strange as it might sound, I always observe what wildlife is doing as I'm making my way to the lake. When those young rabbits are darting through the beams of my morning headlights, I know in my heart that I will start fishing both shallower and a little faster than I would if the rabbits aren't active. If I don't see moving rabbits on my commute, I plan on slowing down and fishing a little deeper to start off with. It's a system I found years ago that is as timeless today as ever. I promise ya, my grandkids and great-grandkids will be watching rabbits on their way to the lake. Pa will see to it! It's a timeless lesson.

Temporarily, let's cast aside (pun intended) any notions about our target smallmouth's audacity and ferocity. This golden fish is as blatantly aggressive as any aggravated Bengal tiger. It lives on its own terms. It doesn't travel far from its happy home, and it has no intentions of letting any living thing interrupt its way of life. It's as territorial as Sitting Bull in the wake of oncoming America. It likes it where it lives. So if you can *find* the fish, you should be able to *catch* the fish.

Finding them is the hardest part

If you find that fish and know he's down there, that fish has only two choices when your bait comes sliding through. He'll either get out of the way, or eat it. Let's hope for number two. You'll soon find out that 50/50 odds are the best you will ever have against Mr. Bronzeback. The odds are almost always in his favor—always. Finding that fish is the hardest part. Ya can't catch 'em until ya find 'em. Uncle Grady taught me that.

Now you know your target and how aggressively territorial he is. If you can find him and aggravate him, he'll tear into your bait like a grizzly. So let's roll up our sleeves and talk about how we're going to accomplish all these things, because it's not just where to go and what to throw—it's whacha do and whacha know. (Somebody grab a guitar!)

How, where, and why are the tough questions I intend to answer in the pages of this book. Basically, there are four factors I'd like to discuss about finding these fish. The remainder of this chapter will cover the things I think will help any angler find smallmouth. I have an age-old method for locating them that I have spoke about in my seminars. These four factors have been my strongholds. They are:

1) **House**
2) **Food Source**
3) **Bottom Conducive to Fish**
4) **Quick Access to Deep Water**

The first we will talk about is what I call the fish's **House**. It's where he lives. Knowing his address will make all the difference.

For instance. In my last book, *Tony Bean's Smallmouth Guide,* I discussed in detail the differences between Largemouth Bass and Smallmouth. I mainly wanted to illustrate that you can't fish at Mr. Largemouth's House if you are looking for Old Man Smallie. You can't use a largemouth bait when fishing for smallmouth — it only makes good sense. Knowing this without question, let's size-up a smallmouth House.

House: When determining key factors in a smallmouth home, we must look at the fact that along with the best House must go a bottom conducive to the fish. The bottom is so important to a smallmouth bass fisherman that one chapter of a book cannot do it justice. As fisherman, we have all crawled or cranked a bait across the bottom and come back with all that mucky looking junk hanging on our hooks.

Have you ever caught a smallmouth bass in that stuff? NOOO! But like the hard-headed fishermen we are, we clean off our hooks and make another cast. By this stage in our fishing careers, we should know better. We should have already started the engine while thinking of our next location for smallmouth houses.

It took me a while to know that the first time that happened to me, it was time to move. This lesson didn't tell me where to fish next, but it told me where *not* to fish. Sometimes knowing where *not* to fish is just as important.

Thinking along these House lines, it's wise to consider how a good House remains good. Just like homes in subdivisions, the smallmouth House retains its value much the same.

For instance, if you live in a nice home in a nice subdivision—and you move—more than likely someone is going to come along and want to purchase your "good House." Smallmouths behave exactly the same way. If one big smallmouth is caught in one of your favorite spots, and he moves (or hits the live well), another will be taking up residence there shortly. Good House is good House. That's lesson one of my four "find them" techniques.

Food Source: The next lesson I managed to teach myself was what our good friend, Mr. Smallie, eats. He's probably going to live close to what's near and dear to his tummy.

What is the favorite food of a smallmouth bass? Crawfish. Where do crawfish go in the winter time? The mud. Where do they come out of in the spring? The mud. Where are we going to fish? Common sense. MUD. This one is House, Food Source, and Bottom Conducive to Fish. They all go hand in hand.

Bottom Conducive to Fish: When talking about smallmouth House mud, I am not talking about mud that you could sink up to your knees in, instead I'm talking about a harder mud mixed in with some gravel. If you can find such a bottom and can mix it with quick access to deep water … you've found a good combination.

Quick Access to Deep Water: When I say quick access, I truly mean quick access. I'm not talking about a mile away. A nice gravelly/muddy flat along a river channel is dead-on perfect ... or a deep hole near mud in the currents of a river. Each have a similar effect on bait fish and their movements. This form of structure has it all. Bait fish school in these deep waters, right near a great crawfish muddy flat. It's the restaurant our golden buddy loves.

Now, we have started to form our pattern to catch smallmouth bass. Knowing that this fish is an opportunistic feeder, you'll realize it can pick and choose between the easiest food sources moving on a particular day. If those schools of minnows are flowing up out of deep water and into the House, that is what is on the menu. If bait fish stop moving, the crawfish just might be a more likely meal. If neither is present, then we, the smallmouth fishermen, provide what that fish thinks it wants in the way of a food source.

That fish might not even be feeding on this day. It might not even be hungry. But keep in mind that 90 percent of fish are not feeding when caught ... **you** make them bite. By placing an interesting food source in front of an aggressive smallmouth, you have effectively *enticed* him into striking.

This theory also illustrates another point. If you are fishing with a minnow ... in a school of minnows ... why would that fish pick *yours* over the million others? Remember that *enticing* part? What if you use a slightly different bait to catch a glance from that fish? Sometimes a "crippled minnow" type of bait looks like a sure and easy meal. That's just a thought to ponder. Would you rather chase a pork chop, or sit down to one already on the table?

Food Source at the House

To illustrate my House point, I'll share a map section which clearly depicts a prime location. It's a map section from a man-made reservoir, but similar conditions can be found in other types of lakes if you use your imagination.

The illustration shows deep water near shallow water and a food source. This illustration has very deep water (old river channel) flowing into a steep bluff, right near a mud and shale flat. The slight current of the old riverbed helps force those baitfish near the flat, thus creating exactly what we've been discussing.

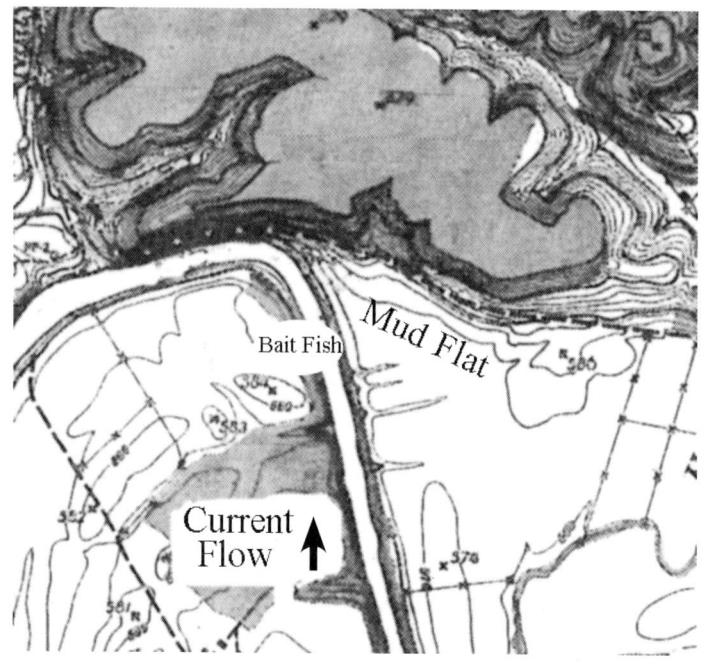

A perfect mud House near deep water

Often times, the bait fish will suspend in this deep water near the bluff of the old river channel—or maybe just a deep section of water nearby. At certain times of the year, like early fall, smallmouth follow these "clouds" of minnows, taking opportunity to feed from below. Those fish love to attack from beneath. If you think about it, it's all about what fish see looking up, not what we see looking down.

Me … finding House.

There are still other times of the year when that same type of baitfish school will ease up onto that flat, primarily late spring. Just when Mrs. Smallmouth leaves her nest bed on that flat, it's conveniently time for those minnows to come knocking on her door. This is another fun time for us fishermen. That's when we toss some sort of minnow bait onto those flats, fishing the shallower and easier waters of the flat. We can toss a fly, swimming it in a minnow type of manner, or get creative with the old tackle box and throw a spoon. There are many options when this feeding frenzy happens.

As you can see, many different things take place in locations like these. It really doesn't matter what month of the year you fish, simply move deeper or shallower when things aren't happening to suit you. If those fish aren't up on that flat in shallow water, they're probably *very* close by in the deeper water—either right on that edge, or suspended out in the deep.

On any given body of water, I can take a simple contour map and circle six spots just like the map I've shown you. By doing that, I greatly reduce the amount of time it takes me to start catching fish. With the individual circles on my map, I try to find places that have all four of my "find them" rules. I've got change in lake bottom contour *(Access to Deep Water)*—I've got bottoms that appear to be right *(Conducive to Fish—Mud)*, and I've got potential for a *Food Source* ... all right there where I can fish it all in a one hundred yard cross-section of lake. I've narrowed my search greatly by finding *House*.

And it's just like me to go knock on the door.

Finding House on a contour map will be far more productive than fishing what looks cool up on shore. The fish don't see what we see.

What they see is House.

CHAPTER TWO

Knocking on the Door of the House

As you might have guessed, four factors are going to be paramount throughout this book. We will continually refer to them, reinforcing their value with each new step we take. It will all mingle, but those four steadfast rules will be the mainstay of our work. Now that you understand the value of the perfect smallmouth House, we will talk about how you're going to get inside. How are we going to implement what we've learned so far? How are you as a fisherman going to get your foot in the door?

Let's knock.

I hate to repeat anything from my first book, so a simple reminder here is enough. We must recognize the difference between the Smallmouth House and the Largemouth House. (Strangely, the Kentucky Spotted Bass likes both and might be in either place, but that's another book altogether.) Let's quickly touch base on the two houses and move on.

If I've studied my maps or have been to a location before, I'll know long before I arrive just how and where I want to knock on that door.

Let's say I've found a mud flat near deep water. Let's say I feel comfortable looking at my map for the underwater conditions at my fishing hole. When I arrive—and at first glance—I notice two types of structure here ... brushy stick piles at a certain depth and a row of stumps in the mud about the same depth. Now I know where to start my casts.

Smallmouth would much rather hang near the bottom (mud bottom) around a stump structure than suspend in the tangled brush of Mr. Largemouth's home. It's a different mind set for each fish. I might throw up in the brush if I'm nearby, thinking that a Spotted Bass might be fun to toy with, but by and large, my main aim is that stump row down where I can't quite see, but know it's there. That shallow brush nearby would just be a quick visit—not a knock on the door.

I'll go knocking over at those stumps first ... *every time!* The point I'm trying to make is that given two identical muddy points on a lake; if one has stumps instead of brush, I'll pick that stumpy point. The brush just isn't as good when it comes to being a smallmouth House.

A common misconception is that smallmouth lock into those stumps and rocks in the mud and hold up there. Not so. The smallmouth bass is a free roaming fish, always checking out his home grounds like a pride lion. He doesn't want any intrusion in his area of influence. He'll run off other fish and spend his time roaming from structure to structure, simply investigating what's coming and going in his neck of the woods. If that something is your grub or fly ... guess what? He'll fight it or eat it. Sometimes both. Again, 50/50 is the best odds you'll ever have as a fisherman, but this angry streak in the smallmouth helps your chances of him striking your bait.

The aggressive four pound smallie pictured on the next page seriously misjudged his prey. The photo shows, if you can make that fish mad, he'll fight. That much is in your favor. Mr.

PHOTO, JESSE WALTON

SOMETIMES SMALLMOUTH CAN BE TOO AGGRESSIVE.
This four-pounder was found floating in Dale Hollow Lake. The Shellcracker was pried from its mouth and the smallmouth lived! The one-pound Shellcracker didn't.

Smallmouth has a bit of an attitude problem. He likes things his way, and he'll sometimes fight when he should "keep his mouth shut". That's a good thing for us fishermen. We can take advantage of his aggression.

I often mention 8´ to 15´ of water depth when advising fishermen where to start. These have always been the magic numbers for me when it comes to smallmouth bass fishing. Whether I'm fishing in an Arizona canyon lake or the grass lakes of the north, I still use this factor for where to begin my search. Even in the deep clear lakes of Tennessee, this depth range has always been a special factor for me.

There are several reasons for this, but before I go any further, I will say that I can adjust very quickly to shallower or deeper feeding fish. Most fisherman have a comfort range where things seem to work the best—this is where you can feel your baits and the bottom better, or you can control your baits to a better degree. That range for me is 8´ to 15´ of water. Yet there is one more reason for this depth, the most important of all, smallmouth bass like these numbers, too.

I have spent many long productive days fishing in the canyon lakes of Arizona. One of these is Apache Lake, located just 40 miles east of Phoenix, Arizona, on the Salt River. Some of the canyon walls reach a 1000´ or more, straight up. If you are running the lake, your depth finder can fall off the scales at 200´ or more, yet 90 percent of the fish in this lake are caught in from 8´ to 15´ of water. The reason, as we said before, is the comfort zone … and fishermen are comfortable fishing these depths. Arizona isn't the only smallmouth heaven on earth, but they sure have their share of feisty smallmouth. I love it there.

Later on in this book we will go into baits, but I want to emphasize one more time … you can't catch fish until you find them, and you will find a lot of fish at these magic numbers. Of course, given certain situations when Mother Nature decrees, these same fish will be shallower or deeper, these are just the magic numbers giving you a place to start.

Now we want to go further and expand on that comfort zone with another factor. It's a very important one: *The Ability to Feel.*

By this, I mean the bait you are fishing, the bottom where you cast, and the subtle vibrations in the rod itself when the bass taps your bait. *Feel* is a *practiced* ability—not one that just comes to you overnight. Remember, *if you can't properly feel the bait, you will never feel the fish when it hits!*

If you remember my comment about "what the fish sees looking up," you'll understand that our five-pounder can make a bound up at minnows in that depth with speed that will astound you. If a school of shad move in around a smallmouth, in a split second he will have his belly bloated full of those minnows. How many bass have you caught in early spring, and before you can even get them to the boat they are spitting up dozens of shad, just trying to cough out that hook? If you catch two on one point, the water will be silver with floating shad. Again, Mr. Smallmouth takes no prisoners. He'll eat until the intruding presence is gone from his neighborhood.

We haven't yet talked about lures and bait, but we will. Right now, though we're going to talk about a big factor in catching and *not* catching bass. It's the ability of the fisherman to *feel* both the bait and the bottom. Of course, each bait and lure has its own special set of characteristics. Each one tugs and pulls in different ways. As a fisherman, you simply must know what your bait feels like when fished properly. If you don't know what that bait is *supposed* to feel like, then you certainly won't know when that bite happens.

A good example of *feel* can be illustrated like this. Let's say we are using an eighth-ounce hair jig (one of my favorites) and casting into about 8´ of water. I've thrown those old jigs enough to know what the bottom is like wherever I fish. I *know* mud from mud-and-shale. I know weed beds from road beds. You will, too, given practice. And ya know why? 'Cause you're going to learn to *feel* that lure.

Feeling the Lure

Many factors come into play with *feel*. Wind, waves, current—all play a huge part. If *current* is your obstacle, you must increase weight in your lure. Re-tie a quarter-ounce jig and *feel* it. If that lure slams into the bottom and drags … it's too heavy. If it never touches bottom, it's too light. Hit the happy medium.

If *wind* is your obstacle in the *feel* game, try this. If your bait is able to touch bottom, but the wind is blowing a huge bag in your line and moving your bait too quickly and without proper presentation to the fish and its bottom—do what I do. Put your rod tip under water. Make your cast, drop the line as quickly as possible, and dip that tip under water. Fish with your rod tip down. Setting your hook can be tricky, but hey … if you never feel that bite, you'll never catch the fish. To even your odds—dip the tip under water.

It's important to realize that wind is not your enemy. It can be a tremendous obstacle in your fight to maneuver your boat, but the wind is not an enemy. It produces fish if we utilize its benefits.

How many of you out there have made casts and just plain couldn't get a feel of the bait? (Raise your hand!) You know … you just can't get your head wrapped around the spot you're fishing. How many of you have looked over at your fishing partner and asked, "Can you feel the bottom? I just can't feel it." And yet, most of us still keep right on fishing. When your brain is asking you questions about *feel*, it's time to listen up and readjust what you are doing.

I can't lie. I raised my hand, too. I'm guilty. I've done it—but I've learned. I know better now. There is absolutely no sense in casting if you are merely tossing line and lure. You're fishing, not practicing your casting skills. Teach yourself to change when your tactics aren't working properly.

Let's talk more about change and why some tactics just don't work. So far, we have talked about depth and *feel* when fishing the House—all very important to a smallmouth bass fisherman. But how we fish these houses is just as important as the House itself. Proper *presentation* is the key to pulling that fish out of his home.

I have an old saying I made up years ago that I think everyone will understand and ponder.

> *If you can hit the bank with your bait, 90 percent of the fish are on the other side of the boat.*

We really need to think about this one. It's big. Almost all of us are guilty at some point of breaking this rule. Here's another saying I use that will make you think, too.

> *The only part the bank plays for a smallmouth fisherman is it keeps all the water from running out of the lake.*

At any given moment, only 1% of the fish in a lake are up near the bank … right up shallow near the shore. About the only reason for the fish to be there in the first place is it probably chased a minnow up there (or your lure). Mother Nature said, "Boys and girls, the bait is up there … chase it."

Cast at the 99 percent group of fish instead of that freak 1 percent up on shore that everyone else has already thrown at. It doesn't matter if there is a House in the middle of the lake on a ten foot hump with no shore nearby. The fish don't care, but we should.

I think we've all been guilty of fishing down a long steep bank where we caught no fish—then going right back and fishing it again just because the old fisherman in our head was telling us *that bank sure looks good*. The fish can't see that gorgeous rocky bank. You and I see it, not them. Maybe it looks like that deeper where the fish *can* see it … and maybe it doesn't. We gotta do our homework to figure out where that fish is and make our casts there. Don't be fooled by that old fisherman in your head. That bank is only pretty for the fisherman—not the fish. Eliminating water is just as important as finding good fishing holes.

Honestly, finding success might be as simple as backing away from the bank a little and fishing farther from the water's edge.

I'm not saying "don't fish the shoreline." I just mean that it's not the only place to cast. There are good spots both near shore and mid-lake. It all goes back to House. Study your House and the reward will be golden (or bronze in the form of a fish!).

Let's look at another bank. We just fished that last long bank with no luck. This bank, however, is somehow different. We caught three good fish here — bang, bang, bang. Now, instead of patting yourself on the back and remembering this spot as a honey hole, sit back and analyze the situation.

You need to answer these questions:

- Why did I catch these fish here?
- What's different about this particular bank compared to the last unproductive one?

Again, grab your map. Study. Are there secondary points beneath the surface you can't see from above? (Remember, it isn't about what *we* see … it's what the *fish* see.)

Something on this bluff or point is different. Smallmouth bass love a House with access to deep water *and* something irregular in the form of structure to relate to (rocks, stumps, slightly different bottom configuration, etc.) If you want to catch more fish today (and I think you do), then look for another spot on your map similar to this one.

Something made this a great location. Figure out what did the trick and remember it. Better yet, mark your map with every note you can. Write right on it (they sell more). Write down today's characteristics, water temperature, depth, wind and whether it was sunny or cloudy. Try to make a magic recipe you can follow to recreate your good fortune. It'll be worth it on your next trip.

Here are some locations I've studied over the years. Although I want to teach you to find recipes of your own, these are tried and true places where you'll find fish:

1) A bank where each end drops into deeper water.
2) A bank where one end or the other meets a shallower flat.
3) A bank with a rocky area jutting out into the lake beneath the surface.
4) Simple humps mid lake with any sort of stumps or grass patches.
5) A change in the tree line up on shore (hardwood tree line meets softwood).

Number five is a great one. Let me elaborate.

Is there an area where hardwood trees like oaks and maples make a defined line on the bank where they meet a stand of softwood trees like pines? While you can't see this under the water, you can bet that Mother Nature did not have a hand in this situation—man did.

In southern man-made reservoirs that have been dammed up, certain things left behind years ago have become homes for lots of fish. If you find these areas, they probably represent an "old home place" as we in the south call them. The defined area was probably a fence row at one time.

That old fence row probably extended out into the water, where the hardwood timber was cut down for the formation of the lake—hence, a stump row or possible change in lake bottom (the irregularities we mentioned earlier).

Keep in mind, if there is a fence row in our special spot, there might have been a house or barn foundation nearby … maybe even a roadbed. All of these are good smallmouth bass spots if you can find them, *and you can*. Most of the maps still show where those houses and barns once stood ... and that's where your boat should be.

Let's get back to wind and how it helps and hinders us all. Remember ... you can fish in the wind. It isn't easy, but it's a technique that many fishermen pass up. Know this. If you hide from the wind, you are probably hiding from the fish, too.

When it comes to feeling a bait in certain places, *boat position* is a big factor. I try to never have to fight the boat for position and fish at the same time. That sounds impossible, but let me explain what I mean. Maybe you say that fishing in the wind is a boat control situation, and that is correct, yet there are easier ways to control your boat that give you better advantage. If all you do is fight the boat, you aren't fishing.

Addressing a bank or certain fishing spot with the wind hitting the side of the boat is difficult. You are constantly adjusting the boat because it continually tries to ride with the wind, going too fast and trying to go shallower at the same time. If you are going down a bank and throwing a crank bait, this may be fine. After all, many of our crank bait casts are nearly parallel to shore anyway. But if you're fishing a one-eighth ounce hair jig with 101 Uncle Josh pork frogs, the game changes.

There is always a spot of neutrality between a boat and the wind. This is hard to explain, but I'll give it a try. Here's what comes into play; we don't want to lose contact with our bait or the bottom if that's where we're fishing, and we do not want that big bag in the line.

To address this, I point the nose of my boat into the wind or to the spot in the wind where the boat seems to be neutral. It's hard to pinpoint that spot, but it's there. This is the spot where the smallest amount of effort is needed to control the boat, nose into the wind and keep the narrowest vantage point for the wind to use you and your boat as a sail.

Practice this the next time you go to the lake. If you can control the boat with as little effort as possible, you'll have more time and energy to fish. You'll have to fish a little differently than usual, but presentation of the bait in the wind is a different game. I'll try to show you how to make your casts with the best results.

I suppose you have always been told not to throw behind the boat. Well, Old Tony's gonna change your thoughts on that one.

Let's say the wind is blowing at a quarter-angle into a cove or creek. If you ride with the wind going into the cove, control of both boat and bait is much harder than it would be if you were cutting into the wind coming out of the cove. Nosing into the wind will slow down the wind's affect on your boat, and give you more time to make good, well-fished casts. This approach coming out of the cove will dictate where you make your casts.

I try to always position myself to make casts at a 45° angle to the boat or even more toward the back of the boat. If I have to … the rod tip goes under the water or I change to a heavier bait like I mentioned before. (Example: One-eighth lead head and grub to a quarter-ounce). It always comes back to controlling your situation. Find a way to *feel* in the wind.

I suppose the main point of this "knock on the door" chapter is that feeling the bottom is huge. Most of my big smallmouth have come off the bottom to bite my lure. Most are living close to their House mud. Aside from some special circumstances at certain times of the year, most are caught near the bottom at the magic depth numbers we discussed. We'll toy with special circumstances in the later chapters, but by-and-large, our golden fish's happy-zones lie in his House ninety percent of the time.

Learn *feel* in the House, and you will increase your odds 100 percent. The next chapter will tell you how to learn that special *feel*.

A Fun Story on *feel*

Back years ago when I was guiding for smallmouth on Percy Priest Lake, just outside of Nashville, I had two clients from Florida who had never caught a smallmouth bass. One caught onto my teachings pretty quick while the other had a hard time. We were fishing one-eighth ounce hair flies on the bottom in 9′ of water. The size was perfect but he didn't understand my spiel and how the whole *feel* thing worked.

As we all know, there will be no clap of thunder or jarring of the rod hard enough to yank your arm out of socket when a fish "taps" the bait.

So I improvised. I told him to watch his line closely, and told him, "If *anything* different happens, set the hook."

Still no results. Poor guy.

Finally, I saw his line twitch and shouted, "Set the hook!"

The fellow did just as he was told, and six pounds of smallmouth bass came to the surface. Three jumps later, she spit out the hook! Simple as that.

He turned to me, all excited and said, (and I quote) "I have part of this figured out. At least now I know what they feel like when they spit it out."

Fun smallmouth days …

CHAPTER THREE

Learning *Feel*

As we have said before, many factors go into the success of a smallmouth bass fisherman. None of those factors are as important as the ability of the fisherman who has taught himself *feel*. The angler who can tell what his bait is doing on the bottom, and what it is encountering while there, is going to out-fish others ten-fold.

So many factors come into play where *feel* is concerned. The ability to feel the bait you are fishing on a bottom and where it *will be the most productive* is the first step to success.

When my Uncle Grady taught me to fish, feel was not a big factor. Back then, I just watched the man's mannerisms. Plus, the rods and reels we were using were not set up for feel, they were more for holding on after the fish took the bait. Some of those big fish in the river need some strong equipment just to land them in the boat.

As I progressed in my fishing, I became aware of just how important *feel* is. We've talked about *feel*, but now we need to discuss how a fisherman learns to *feel*. How does he or she gain that knowledge?

Here's the way I taught my son ... and how he then taught his friends.

A good place to learn is a creek. I refer back to creeks often because there is so much to learn there. Consider that clear creeks have all of the bottoms you would find in any lake. With those clear waters allowing you to see what's beneath the surface, you can visualize what's going on and practice a certain amount of visual learning that way. These waters also give us avenues to learn *without* seeing bottom, too! This is a fun lesson.

How to Start

When on the creek with your fishing buddies, pick a location to begin some test casts. While standing in the same spot, cast into the open water areas where you can see the bottom. Drag, or I should say *work,* your bait across the bottom and *feel* through your rod. *Feeling* the bait, and seeing how that bait is reacting when it touches a certain object or is being worked on a certain bottom is an important lesson. Repeat this process until you feel comfortable that you have a good idea of the bottom contours and the obstacles your bait came in contact with. Then move to another location with different bottom features and do it again.

My suggestion would be to test a gravel bottom, a mud bottom, a gravel *and* mud bottom, and bottoms that change from one to the other.

Pull your bait over rocks of different sizes and into wood or grass—*learning feel.* I would suggest spinning tackle with no more than eight-pound test line. I'd also suggest that you use a lead-head at first, probably a quarter ounce with a grub attached. Bend the hook back into the grub so as not to get hung up. You are learning, not fishing at this point.

If you get a strike, that will also be a learning experience—telling the subtle differences between a bump on a log and a thump

Bumping a rock or other object with the bait alerts a smallmouth that food is on the way. Usually, the bass will be positioned on the downstream side of the cover and the bait should be presented from the upstream side. Illustration by Lenny McPherson

from a fish strike. Plus, it's fun watching those bass peck away at the bait, frustrated that they just can't take it with them!

The grub gives perhaps the best natural feel for learning. I would suggest that you use this method only in places where you can see the bottom and can tell for sure what you're are learning to *feel*. You are learning the exact feel of what you can see. Your eyes are seeing the bottom—and your brain is reacting to that stimuli. You need to see what the bait is moving over in order to add to your skills.

Now, here's where it gets interesting.

As I did with my son—and he did with his friends—add a blindfold to the scenario.

While all these different stimuli are still fresh in your brain, use that blindfold to extract what you've learned—both consciously and unconsciously. Cast in different directions, testing different locations, this time using only *feel*.

What you have learned changes once you use the blindfold. You could say that it's just like fishing in deeper water where *feel* is the only avenue you'll be able to utilize.

With the blindfold in place and your eyes out of the picture, the feel of the rod in your hands is telling the brain what is happening. It's processing *feel*.

When it's your turn, tell your buddy what type of bottom you're *feeling*. When you do, let your fishing buddy recast and repeat the process. You will be quite surprised at the results. It's as if *feel* changes once you can't see where you're fishing.

This is not something you're going to master in one outing to the creek or even several trips to the lake, but it's one you must master in order to change your percentages of fish caught—not through luck, but through your patience and understanding of any given situation.

I don't think that on your first trip with the blindfold that you will need to know the difference between the *feel* of gravel and 3″ river rock—or even big rock to boulders. These more complex conditions will come into play with practice and experience. What you need to learn on your first trip is the difference between a muddy, mucky bottom and one that will hold fish.

In order to be successful at the lake, you need to know the difference between a bottom conducive to fish and one that holds no life at all. It's as if the muddy, leafy, mucky junk you're *feeling* has no life to transmit back through the rod—while the gravelly bottom is sending subtle hints through the rod at all times.

With a little knowledge, your degree of confidence will increase. When this happens, your fun on the water catching fish will be magnified and you'll have a much more joyful experience rather than just another day on the water.

"I believe that I can catch a five pound smallmouth bass every time I make a cast." I've said that many times in the classes I've taught across the country. Of course, I don't always catch that big

Jay and his friend using the Blindfold Method to learn FEEL.

beauty on those casts, but I *believe* I can. The day I stop believing is the day my smallmouth bass fishing is over for good.

This blindfold method may sound a little far-fetched, but if you test it properly, I truly believe it will help your future fishing ability. It improves proper retrieve, it creates confidence, and it will help you maintain those 50/50 odds we're all trying to achieve in this old smallmouth puzzle we're trying to solve. It's a major tool.

Reggie Smith holding a gorgeous 5+ pounder.

CHAPTER FOUR

Sales Pitch

Now that we've found our smallmouth *House* and have our foot in the door, we need to find ways to ensure that our smallmouth takes the bait. We need to be certain that once in the door, we can make a presentable sales pitch to our smallmouth like we're door-to-door salesmen pitching buy lines.

We've found the door and knocked, now we need to sell our product properly. We must make the correct *presentation* of our lure to the fish and do it in ways that will increase our odds of making a sale. To illustrate my point, I'd like to cover some dos and don'ts of casting.

Often times, a fisherman has found the House with all the right things to hold a smallmouth, but he fails to make the right types of casts to gain the fish's attention. The fish is there, but the cast misses him completely.

I see fishermen making poor casts at my seminars all the time. I'm talking about talented pole-handlers who fail once the bait hits that perfect X-marks-the-spot. Have you ever made a perfect cast and immediately closed your bail and tightened the line? If you could see what happens beneath the waves, you might be surprised. With your line tight before the bait hits bottom, the tension in the line will tug the bait back closer to the boat, pulling it away from your target. When you do this, Mr. Bass never sees your presentation.

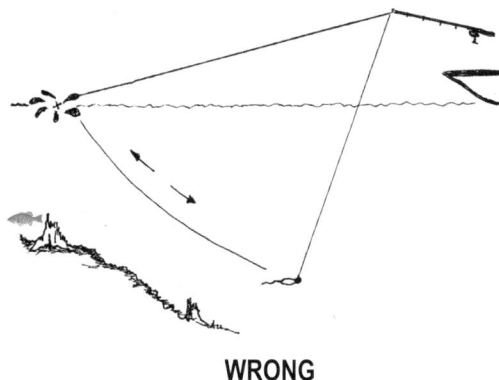

WRONG

Never hold too much tension after the cast is made. This might work at certain times of year, but most conditions call for a different approach.

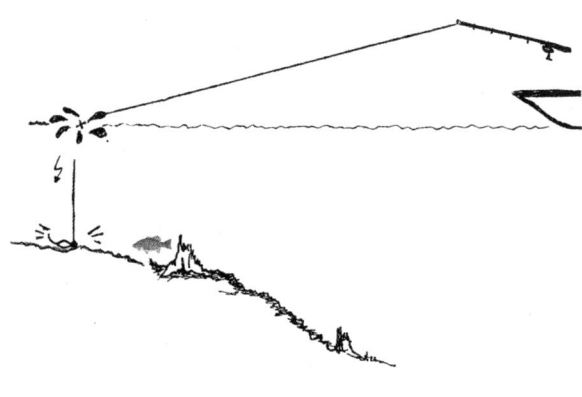

RIGHT

Try to cast beyond your target point and allow your bait to fully hit bottom before you close the bail and start your retrieve.

Another crucial mistake (even if you let the bait hit bottom) is tightening your line and immediately raising your rod tip. Keep in mind, if your bait has dropped into the House and you pull your rod tip up 5´—your bait just swam 5´ to 10´ out of the House.

Ten feet may not sound like much, but if that smallmouth isn't active today, it might as well be 50´. You'll need to drop it on his nose and be patient. What's the use of making a perfect cast if you're going to immediately pull your bait 5´ away? You might as well just click your bail and throw the bait by hand.

Let the bait sit there for a little bit. Twitch it if you want, but be patient. Don't step back out of the door, you're a salesman. If you're fishing a tube or craw, the longer the bait stays in the strike zone, the better. If you're fishing a swimming type of bait like a grub, the cast should be far beyond your target so when your bait swims past the smallmouth House you have total and complete control of it. You have *feel* at that crucial moment. *Feel* is crucial here.

With these two don'ts out of the way, I'd like to cover some do's. We're going to call this next lesson: *Casting Patterns for Testing an Unknown Spot.*

I use a specific pattern when approaching a spot I've never fished. I've never been there before, but I already have a pretty good idea of where the fish will be. I use the simple test cast pattern below to properly present my bait to the fish so I don't miss him or spook him before I have the opportunity to catch him.

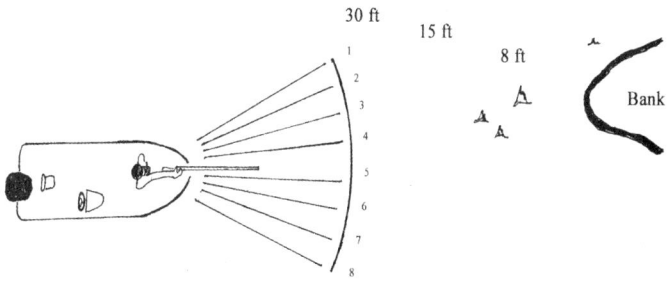

Notice the particular depths and the locations of the stumps on this point I'm about to test. Many fishermen would start on one side of this point and work around to the other, casting the bottom. Not me. I want to know if that fish is active and suspended a little, or sluggish and hugging close to cover. Here's how I start my test.

I start my casting procedures with my boat farther out than most fishermen. If I slide in too close right off the bat, I could spook fish in deeper water. I don't know where that fish is hanging out today. I don't know if he's in shallow water, deep water, suspended or hugging the bottom. By systematically eliminating each of these conditions, I can find that first fish and zero in on where the next one might be.

Remember when I told you that when we can reach the shore with our casts, 90 percent of the fish are on the other side of the boat? That's exactly what I'm trying to illustrate here. It's my hope that I'm reaching 15′ of water with my cast. I've studied my map. I've pondered this spot long before I start casting.

I've wanted to be here "in my head" long before my boat idled into this spot. I have a plan long before arrival. I want to hit that deep water first. My boat might be in 45′ of water. It might be in 25. If I've studied my contour map properly, I'll know how deep it is at my target spot.

This example is only one of many. I can see the lines on the map like everyone else. This is merely an example of *one* type of target place where this can be used. Every spot changes, of course, but our map will help us judge those unknown and unfished spots.

Depending on what my map says, I will strategically cast into 15′ first. I might even cast into even deeper water. Remember, this is strategic. I am starting deep and working my way up. If the fish are shallow, I'll get to them eventually. If they are deep,

I won't be caught with my pants down—up too shallow beating the water to a froth. It's strategic. It's smart fishing.

It's what *you* need to do in your process of elimination. Start deep and work your way up shallow. No rush. Fish this spot right. Dozens of anglers slap at the shores and move ... then slap at the shores again. Fish each spot properly before you start moving that boat. Diligence will produce fish. Fish what you *don't see*!

Aside from all other things, I have one technique that very few anglers use. It's simple and easy. It's step number one in the test-casting process. Hear me on this one! I do it on *every* new spot. If I've never been there, I always hit it the same way. I start my process.

Step one is throw a top water bait into the spot. I make three strong casts (boat in slightly deeper water so I can't reach shore) with a Zara Spook. That old Spook has been a mainstay for me for years. It's my bait, but you may find ones you like better. When I find something that works, I stick to it like glue. I cast out that Spook the first three times. This accomplishes at least two things. One, it tells me if the fish are active, hungry and feeding top water. Two, these types of baits allow me to cast farther than my jigs will reach. I'm covering more ground with less effort.

A NOTE ON ZARA SPOOK

The first bait I use in my test patterns is the Zara Spook. I usually make no more than three casts each side of the point and the top. If I catch a fish ... that's great. If a fish comes up and misses the bait, that's okay, too. Now I know that he or she is there (accomplishing my first step goal ... assessing how active the fish is).

Let's move on, assuming the Spook did not produce. The next bait I pick up is the grub (in later chapters, we will go into sizes and colors). I make no more than eight casts in a fan cast motion into the same depth where the Spook was hitting. I allow the bait to touch down ... and with a slow and steady retrieve, swim the bait back to the boat as if it were a swimming minnow, not going down the ledge (that is another pattern we will discuss later). Be sure to let the grub sink with an open bail until it touches down, but watch the line as it falls. Lots of strikes occur on the fall. If the grub produces no strikes, I lay that pole down and pick up a bottom working bait.

With the next step, the same eight fan casts work perfectly, only this time ... working the bait on the bottom will work a portion of the drop itself—but not much . The boat has remained in the same position over deep water this entire time.

Now, I move my boat to where the grub cast was hitting the water—and repeat the same process with all of the same baits. This time, I am probably fishing from 8´ to 15´ (and you know how much I like those numbers).

My next move is to the 8´ of water where I can probably reach the bank with all of the baits I've tried, fishing the bottom with the same type of eight casts in a fan shape.

The last step is to fish the bottom and raise the bait off the bottom between tugs, giving the bait a different appeal to the fish.

Now that these steps have been implemented, we can safely ease the boat closer to shore and cast into shallower water. Start with step one and repeat the process. Grab that top water pole and give your three casts. When that boat moves position, you change poles and repeat.

Note: *During excessive wind, I skip this step—but then and* **only** *then. Top water baits are rarely successful in turbulent water. I've seen it happen, but it's rare. I* *try to make every cast count in every weather condition. Knowing your bait and its attributes will save time and energy, especially on a windy day.*

I know that this sounds like a long process and it does take time ... but the results can benefit you in many ways. Do you have to repeat the process every time you go to this point? No, because the pattern you tried has told you many things.

Example: Let's say that while you were trying this pattern you caught three fish in the same spot on the right side of the point in what you now know is 8´ of water on the grub swimming just off of the bottom. *Those fish were there for a reason.* Everything was right. It could be three stumps, or a big rock—or even—dare I say ... a small brush pile?

The next time you go to the same spot, instead of going through all of the same test patterns your first casts *could* be on the spot where you caught them the time before. How will you know the spot? Because when you finished fishing there the first time, you stopped and took the time to make a record of the bait, the depth, the water color, wind direction, bottom features and even the cover or structure nearby.

I know this sounds like a lot of work, and that's why I always have a tape recorder Velcroed to the dash of my boat. I just talk to it and transfer my notes when I get home. If you do this all year long, next year will be a whole new ball game in your fishing days. Is it a lot of work? Yes, but how much is a six pound smallmouth bass jumping around on the end of your line worth?

When I catch a fish (especially in these untested spots), I document my catch. I hold these factors in my head until I can get to my log book. Some fishermen have journals, and some have computer programs. I don't care how you do it, but DO IT!

Your brain won't remember as well as you think it will. There are too many points and coves in your head already. Quite simply:

DOCUMENTATION = FUTURE FISH

Every piece of information you can write down, do it. Some fishermen write journal entries, telling what they did that day and with whom. It's pleasant on a hot August day to sit in the air conditioning and read about that fun day you had with your fishing buddy last November. You'll learn a little with each entry, and you can bet that every salesman who's made a sale has documented it! Once he gets his foot in the next door of the next House, he'll throw that same line (pun intended).

Another thing to ponder is what happens with two fishermen in the boat. If fisherman number one is implementing Step 1, then fisherman number two can proceed to Step 2. This cuts down the time it takes to test a spot. In a matter of one minute, two fishermen can effectively test a location (before moving in closer for round two). It's not rocket science. It's just a really great and simple process that produces smallmouth.

> **NOTE:** *During windy conditions, boat placement can be difficult. We will cover that in a future chapter. But remember ... the wind is not your enemy. She's just a tiger that's tough to tame. On your side, she'll produce more fish for you than just about any other fishing condition.*

A fun story on documentation

I'd like to tell this short story to make my point about documentation. On Percy Priest Lake, just outside of Nashville, Tennessee, I had the pleasure of having one of the finest people that I have ever met in the boat with me. One morning, Al Lindner (*Infisherman* magazine) and I went out after smallmouth.

That morning, I pulled our boat up on a very good smallmouth point. (I had been there and documented my data numerous times). Upon my instruction, Al made a cast to where I pointed.

After no strike on the Zara Spook that I forced him to use, I turned to him and said, "You were eight feet too far to the left."

He grinned and offered his playful smile. "Show me."

I made my cast and let the ripples from the bait disperse. After only three turns of the reel, the bottom came out from under the bait! And after a fairly short but fun fight, a six pound-plus smallmouth bass came to the boat.

Ol' Al turned to me with a grin and said, "You knew that spot, didn't ya?"

One cast—one stump in 6´ of water—one beautiful bass.

You can do the same. Just KEEP RECORDS.

Ask Al … he'll back me up on this one.

*"There are two things
I want to always remember…
My last smallmouth, and my son's first."*

~Tony Bean

CHAPTER FIVE

High/Low Barometric Pressure and Its Effects on Area of Influence

Heavy dew in evening or early morning is a sign of high pressure.

We spoke about *Area of Influence* in an earlier chapter, but we'll touch on it again. Basically, *Area of Influence* is the room a smallmouth occupies on any particular day. Sometimes that fish will have a much larger roaming area than others. There will also be days when the fish just won't be moving, and he'll be nestled in tight to his structure in the House. Many things determine the distance a fish is likely to travel on any given day. One of these things is barometric pressure.

I've often heard fishermen say things like, "The sun is just too bright to catch fish today." It may be true that fishing will be difficult on these particular days, but a more accurate statement might be, "The pressure is high today and the fish are holding tight to structure." Let me try to explain how and why this happens.

Our friend, the smallmouth, has a very delicate system. His equilibrium is governed by an air sack that helps him maintain negative buoyancy. It's his way of *not floating or sinking*. On days that have high pressure, the fish's air sack is under that same high pressure. This makes him lethargic. It's the equivalent of humans experiencing sinus problems. When our sinus cavities are under pressure, we tend to feel sickly and want to hug the couch all day. That's what's happening to fish on these high pressure days. They are hugging the couch in the House.

Understanding this simple principle allows us to learn how to catch fish on these days. For instance, if I know the sun is bright and the water is calm (high pressure), I will slow down my methods of fishing. What I want to do is make each cast count by strategically trying to fish the House in the dead center where that lethargic fish is resting.

If I want to catch him today, I've got to swim that bait right up to him and wiggle it. Just like we learned in the old fable, *The Tortoise and the Hare*: slow and steady wins this race on high pressure days. That fish might not bite your lure today anyway, but this method is the only way you'll entice him off the couch. Slow and easy on high pressure days. Be the Tortoise, not the Hare.

> **Note:** by using Feel, *you can tell when you've tapped that stump or underwater structure. Don't be afraid to let the bait sit a little. You are in the House. It's where you want to be. Too many fishermen get in a hurry for the next cast. Stay put! You're home!*

On the opposite end of the spectrum, low pressure days are days when bass love to move. They are much more aggressive since they're feeling good. They're probably hungry, too, from resting and not eating during high pressure the day before.

I love to fish those days following a high pressure day. I know those fish are hungry. I know they are active. I know that my bait doesn't have to be so precise in the *Area of Influence*. He's gonna come find it wherever it is in his *Area of Influence* and eat it. That is exactly what's on his mind ... EAT IT! It's in his area. He's hungry. That little grub has intruded on his space. Low pressure—you will come to love it.

We've all heard that familiar line, "You should've been here yesterday. They killed 'em." I'd bet "yesterday" was a low pressure day, and it probably followed a high pressure day. If you know why pressure helps and hinders, it will increase your odds many times over. Remember that 50/50 rule? We're still struggling to reach 50 percent.

Whew! This fishing is a lot of pressure!

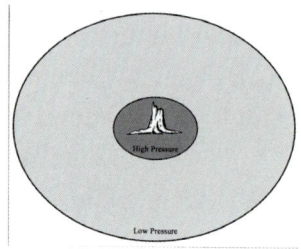

When fishing on low pressure days, it's always good to keep an eye on the sky. Storms are often lurking on these days. Noticing the tell-tale signs is the difference between getting back to the dock and getting drenched!

Face into the wind and storms will be on your right. In this Hemisphere, low pressure winds swirl counter-clockwise.

Fowl tend to fly lower on low pressure days. High pressure affects their ears.

Smoke rises on high pressure days, while it settles downward on low pressure days.

High clouds won't rain on you, no matter how threatening they look. Only low-lying clouds drop rain.

CHAPTER SIX

Baits—The Salesman's Product

Throughout the first few chapters, we've spent a lot of time discussing how to locate smallmouth bass, the kind of structure they live on, and the depth of water they prefer. We've also touched on approach and the methods you should use with certain baits in order to start forming patterns. We've talked about methods of recording those patterns and how important it is to be diligent in maintaining that record book for future fishing trips. All of these concepts are very important components in the master puzzle of the Smallmouth House.

Now we're going to talk about the salesman's product—*bait*. We will also take it a step further and talk about how to correctly fish the baits needed to be successful at smallmouth bass fishing.

You will find that the techniques we're going to discuss here will work equally well with other species of fish that occupy the same water. Many times I've been on a good smallmouth bass hole and a big largemouth bass would race up and take the bait (pun intended). Crappie, walleye, perch—just about any species of fish will succumb to this style of fishing if it's implemented properly.

For example, many years ago when I was guiding smallmouth bass trips on Percy Priest Lake I had one of those special days when my son, Jay, was in the boat with me. We were fishing some of the successful smallmouth holes I'd recorded over the years (documentation).

Jay had already taken two smallmouth bass over 5 pounds and some smaller fish while I was doing everything I could to see that he had a good trip. We were fishing a clear-amber 3" pepper grub on a one-eighth ounce lead head. All at once, Jay's line stretched, and after a few jumps and a very good fight, a 7 ½ pound largemouth gave up and came to the boat.

This fish came out of 14′ of water off of a group of stumps. The date was April 16, 1983—my son was 16 at the time. He also took a 34 pound striper with that grub, along with another five pound smallmouth. What a great day!

See how important my records have been to me? Look at all that information just begging to be used another day. And you know what? It's a wonderful memory, too. Keep records—you'll find they're valuable for more than just fishing information.

Jay and his dandy Largemouth

While the baits we're going to discuss are primarily for smallmouth, a new world of fishing will open up for you with many other species. Good fishing methods are just good, that's all. Practice them regularly, and your success will improve with each outing.

Grubs and Hair Jigs

In all of my years of smallmouth bass fishing, I have relied on the grub in many instances, and it's paid off. The grub is a versatile bait and can be fished in many ways. Although we've already touched on the swimming technique, I want to carry this technique even further to illustrate just how versatile and effective this mainstay jig and grub can truly be. It's always been the "Old Standby" for me.

> **Note:** *The following suggestions apply to hair jigs as well, but for ease-of-read, I will refer to them all as grubs. There are some subtle differences between both baits, but for most measurable means, these two can be lumped together for discussion.*

Swimming the Grub:

Swimming a grub has by-far been one of the largest fish producers for me. The name tells the story—throw it out and swim it back—but there is much more to this little piece of fishing dynamite than merely casting and reeling. If done correctly, this simple bait can be deadly!

We talked a lot about *feel* in the previous chapters. (I know I keep coming back to that, but it's a huge factor.) *Feel* of the grub is all-important. Remember, if you can't *feel* the *bait*, you can't *feel* the *fish* when it hits.

Feel with a grub is connected to the size of lead head you use on the bait. In order to swim the grub properly, *feel* and *control* must come into play. As I said earlier, wind and current will force you to decide what size lead head to use.

Here's a good example. I am fishing in six to 10´ of water with an eighth ounce lead head and a 3˝ grub. I will make a cast and allow the bait to sink to the bottom on a slack line. Once the bait touches down, I'll pick the rod tip up and start my retrieve at the same time (same time … remember this.). This allows me to pull my bait off the bottom just enough to ensure I'm not dragging the bottom as I go.

Since 90 percent of the big bass taken are caught on or near the bottom, what we want the grub to do is to track just off the bottom, while following the contour of the bottom as much as possible. This applies to tapering flats more than any other place.

The reason you start your retrieve at the same time that you pick up the rod tip is to *control* the bait. If you do the same thing every time, when you hook a fish, you'll know *and remember* exactly what you were doing at the time. *Control* of the situation is the key. Practicing the same ritual with each cast will help teach you *feel*. Be consistent.

Speed

I am often asked, "How fast do I retrieve?" That's a good question, and one not easy to answer with words on paper. I could show you by hand with the greatest of ease, but telling the tale in black and white is much more difficult. I can help you control the speed of your bait in a short discussion.

The speed which you use to fish a grub is determined in two ways. One is the type of terrain you are fishing (how deep and how steep). Two is about how aggressive the fish are on this given day. Let's consider fishing the same flat we just discussed. If we start deeper on the flat first (like we discussed in the test pattern), then we'll need to fish slower than we would if we'd moved in closer to shallower water. In shallow water, our bait will hit bottom much quicker than in the deeper areas.

In most all cases, I start with a slow, steady retrieve. A good rule of thumb is this: if you start out slow and the fish are aggressive, you can probably speed up the retrieve. When you're in shallow water (4´ to 8´), still allow the grub to touch down on the bottom on a loose line, but start with the rod tip already in the ten o'clock position. You'll be better able to *control* the bait immediately in the shallower water situation.

As you move into deeper water, remember that *feel* and adjust your fishing. You may want to change the size of your lead head from an eighth to a 3/16 or a ¼ ounce. *FEEL, FEEL, FEEL*, and do not lose *control* of the bait.

If you're swimming the bait too fast to keep it from touching bottom, you probably need to lighten your tackle to a smaller jig size. Slow and easy usually wins this race, but you must be in the right depth regardless.

These last suggestions on speed of retrieve have been conducted on a shallow flat which tapers somewhat, but not drastically. These conditions will make it considerably easier to learn the technique. If you're just now learning to properly swim a grub or hair jig, I suggest a terrain with little elevation change. This allows you to learn your technique and truly get a handle on how the bait will react to your stimuli.

Again, if you are honestly trying to learn how to fish this simple but paramount bait, be consistent in the early stages of your learning curve. What I mean is, don't fish a calm flat, then race to a windy rock bluff, then to a weed bed. Practice in a swimming pool, a shallow flat, or even a bluff—but keep it consistent so you don't go home frustrated with Ol' Tony and his jig-fishing methods. I want you happy. I want you catching fish. I've done it and I know you can, too.

Learn this fish-producing method on a muddy flat. Nearly every lake has one. Find it—fish it—stay there for hours learning *feel*. If your bait hits the bottom now and then, you know that you are learning. Every cast doesn't have to be perfect. Learn from your minor mistakes and elevate your grub fishing ability. That mud flat is perfect to learn on. You'll know when you get it right ... a little fishy will tell you.

Another good point to ponder is this: many fishermen fish a grub or jig with all sorts of gyrations. They bounce that rod tip, they pull and tug and let their line go slack, they wiggle and bump and dance that jig all over the place. You will lose *feel* this way.

Minnows and crawfish don't dance for the fish, and neither should your bait. Keep controlled tension on your grub so you know when you hit weeds, stumps, or even fish. That lifeline of monofilament is your ticket to success. I'll say it again. *That lifeline of monofilament is your ticket to success.* FEEL.

> **NOTE:** *While minnows and crawfish do not dance on the bottom, many fish have been caught on the "bounce the rod tip and hop the bait" method. That is a completely separate technique of fishing covered in later pages in this book.*

Control Depth

Sometimes, fish that are more active come off the bottom to feed in different depths. Here is where *control* is even more important.

Let's say that you're fishing with the grub where the depth is constant at 15´. You've already fished just off of the bottom with the swimming technique. Now, you want to fish at a different level to test the water, so to speak.

Let's say that you want the grub to swim at 8´ in a constant retrieve. Guessing at the depth is one way to do this, but there is another more effective method. I call it the *Countdown Method*, and here is how it works.

Cast your grub and on a loose line count until it hits the bottom. Let's say, for example, it takes a ten-count for the bait to reach the bottom. Retrieve the bait and cast again. When you get to a five-count, start your retrieve. The bait should be swimming halfway between the surface and the bottom.

By the way, on the countdown cast, start with your rod tip at the ten o'clock level and leave it there throughout the entire retrieve. This will keep your bait at a constant level most of the way back to the boat before the up-travel in the line causes the bait to come much shallower. If fish are anywhere below the depth that you're swimming the countdown grub, the odds of bringing them up to your bait are very good. *Remember, it's what they see looking up—not what we see looking down.*

Trust the speed you're choosing, yet re-evaluate your casts. Every reel is different. Practice is extremely important in your learning curve. That's why I can't tell you to crank this speed or that, because each has its own characteristics. My first speed is almost always slow and steady, and I adjust from there.

Here is a method one of my students uses (he told me how he did it). He tested his retrieve and practiced in one place for hours. He learned his "near the bottom" countdown technique by dropping the rod tip a little *during the retrieve* and making his countdown. If the bait hit the bottom immediately, he knew he was just off the bottom where he was supposed to be. If it took a few seconds … he was cranking too fast. He made his adjustments and fished the same spot over and over until he got it.

Practice is the key to learning the *Countdown Method*. You must trust the way you are counting down, and you must trust your cast and your retrieve. It's as important to know what the count is as it is to know where the bait is. Trust yourself and your method.

Here is another good way to learn the *Countdown Method*. Go to the lake with your buddy. Take your graph or flasher and find 15´ of water and drop a buoy. Back off that spot and start to cast until you hit the right distance where you make a good and comfortable cast. Drop another buoy, or better yet, anchor the boat. Tie on a lead head and the grub of your choice, cast and do your count. Repeat this casting until you become comfortable with your count cadence.

Do this with different size lead heads and different size lines. Write down the numbers and study them while you're sitting around the house thinking about fishing. When you feel content at 15´, move your boat into 10´ and repeat the process. This all takes practice and time, but it'll be worth it.

This particular counting method works the best in water no deeper than 20´, and it works extremely well in water 8´ to 15´ deep. My magic numbers have always been 8´ to 15´, and yours can be, too, once you learn to *control* your bait.

There are all kinds of variables with this method, and only you will know in your particular fishing situation which works best. Learn the count and trust it. I do, and it doesn't matter if I'm in Tennessee or Arizona or on the moon for that matter. When chasing smallmouth bass, the count is always on my mind.

Why did I learn this method and where can it help me?

Here are a couple of examples I've used on many occasions.

- There are times when I cross a lake, and I start marking shad 15´ deep with fish just below them. I want my bait to be at 15´. I can do this because I know the count.

- I'm in an area where the grass comes up off the bottom at 10´. I want my bait to swim just above the grass. I can do this because I know the count.
- I mark a school of fish at 15´ and I want my first cast to count, it will because I know the correct count to put my bait right in front of the fish's face. *I'll just bet they'll be looking up at it!!!!*

Note: *In order for the* Countdown Method *to work, you must know the depth of the area where you're fishing and how fast your bait falls. One way to practice this is to check the particular depth of the spot before you fish the area.*

An even better method is to use a swimming pool with a depth in one end of 12´ or 15´. You can practice there to learn your bait's rate of fall with different sizes of lead heads and *watch it happen.*

Once you've done the Countdown Method *a few times, it will become more natural and the counting won't be as necessary. The process becomes second nature.*

A reaffirming way to check your skills is to keep records of your types of casts and the depths you've fished. It's one more way that documentation can help your fishing technique. If the speeds and bait weights aren't working today, you'll have it documented and can reflect on it, try to figure out why, then change your strategy next time.

I'll offer one more group of ideas on *feeling* the grub and making it swim properly. The weight of the jig head isn't the only method you can use to change and control your depth. We also have line varieties and different pound-tests to govern speed and control. Heavier lines will slow the speed of your grubs and change the way you fish different size jig heads. Sometimes a quarter ounce grub on heavier line can be fished faster than a light jig with light gauge line. More than likely, you will find a happy medium and will use one more than the others. You will, however, need to keep different varieties of jigs and lines to use when testing a spot during different weather conditions.

As complicated as much of this sounds, it probably isn't as tough as you're thinking. A few combinations of lines and grubs will teach you what you want to know.

Unfortunately, we can't buy jigs and grubs like we can crank baits. Crank baits and jerk baits often come boxed with labels stating 30´ or 15´. With a grub, it's you, the fisherman, who governs the depth in which you fish. It's all on your shoulders to *control* the grub at whatever speed and depth necessary to catch fish.

Practice your counts and you've just stamped that grub package with 15´ or 8´. You've done your homework with your salesman's product ... bait.

Now, go make a sale.

A beautiful, extra-dark colored smallmouth.

Carl Haley and a beautiful 4+ pounder.

"Parting is Such Sweet Sorrow" and one of the greatest feelings a true smallmouth lover will ever experience.

"All of man's possessions fade away the instant a smallmouth breaks through the surface, sending sparkles of water into a morning sun— the fish connected to the line, to a rod, to a reel in your hand."

*~ **Tony Bean***

CHAPTER SEVEN

A Short Note on Rods and Reels

There are as many rods and reels as there are hairs on a dog's back. Let me try to cover a few simple lessons on each.

Spinning gear is my main choice for smallmouth bass fishing, especially with the small pieces of bait we've been talking about (jigs, grubs, etc). Spinning reels were made for smallmouth and light line fishermen. They are also easier to control when casting into the wind.

I want a spinning reel that states 6, 8, or 10 lb. test line on the box. Your favorite tackle store will have an inventory of rods and reels that will boggle the mind. Choose one with this light-line listing. Most good reels will have these digits stamped on the spool. You'll need a good light-line reel for fishing the small jigs and grubs we've discussed. Also, ask your friendly tackle shop salesman about reels with a smooth drag. When using light line and tackle, a smooth drag is essential.

Usually, you can load about 150 yards of 8 lb. test onto these reels. Never load a spinning reel past 1/8 of an inch from the top of the spool. Too much line means too many problems. Also, when loading line on a spinning reel, always let the line come from the top of the spool spinning toward you out of the box. Never lay it on the floor and start filling your reel spool. This can cause all kinds of problems with kinks and knots in your line while fishing. It twists the line before you even get a chance to get it wet.

When it comes to what kind of line to use, I'm of the old school—I'm a monofilament man. I know monofilament stretches much more than the new braids, and the abrasive resistance is far less than the new line—but monofilament line is my thing ... and for many reasons.

When I'm on the water fighting a big smallmouth bass, the fight means more to me than bringing the fish to the boat in a hurry. I want to see the jumps and feel the stretch on the line as it spins through the spool, working the drag. You can't underestimate monofilament. Just think of all the fish that were caught using this old standby line!

But alas ... one-day monofilament will go the way of the Dodo Bird. The new braids and polycarbonates are, in fact, superior to monofilament, but the stretch of monofilament helps that hook stay set.

Braided line, though superior in many ways, has very little stretch and can have an adverse effect on the smallmouth characteristic head shake. One little shake of the head can jerk a hookset from its jaw.

A little stretch isn't a bad thing. Old School loves monofilament. Let this old bass fisherman have his fun and stick with the monofilament that has helped bring a young boy to the keys of this computer, writing this book for you. Ask around—get all the information that you can on all the different types of line and then make your own decision.

*Note the proper bend of the rod tip.
20% tip bend, 80% backbone.*

The rod you use is your connection to the *feel* of the bait and the strike. Or in the case of the smallmouth, it's that subtle, almost undetectable bump. I prefer a six-foot rod with a very sensitive tip and lots of backbone. This is what I call a 20/80 … twenty percent tip and eighty percent backbone. Remember that the backbone of a rod sets the hook while the tip allows you to feel the bite. Don't get confused when looking at a rod and say that the tip is too weak. It just may be *reel* sensitive (yet another pun).

I like a six-foot rod. There are many reasons why, but I feel that I have the maximum amount of control I need to cast, feel, set the hook, and fight the fish. Backbone for strength—sensitive rod tip for feel. 20/80. It's that simple.

James Blair holds a beautiful 6+ pound smallmouth bass. James has been a lifelong fishing buddy and an excellent smallmouth fisherman.

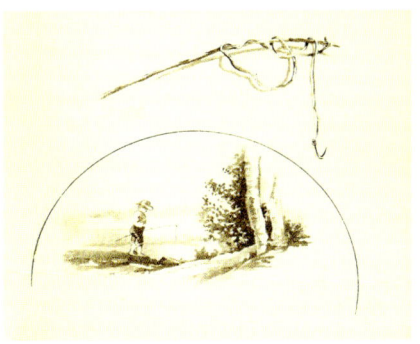

CHAPTER EIGHT

Creeks Were Made to Wade

Some of my best memories of youth are of the times I spent in the creeks where I lived. However, at that time I had no idea that these wandering streams would start a lifetime of fishing most fishermen can only dream of. As an adult, I've been so fortunate to be able to live and breathe Smallmouth bass fishing during my years on Earth. But as a kid … wading those old streams *set the hook* for me the rest of my life.

When I was very young, my Uncle Grady would take me to the rivers and lakes in our area—mostly because he knew I would throw a fit if he didn't. My uncle was a good fisherman; he didn't go after giant records or fish the big tournaments like I did, but he did put in many man-hours of fishing just for the pure enjoyment of the sport.

Many times I watched him stand in the same place on the banks of Woods Reservoir and throw a live minnow (or one of those old-style artificial worms we had back then) into a hole of water while I was running up and down the bank testing out every inch of the water and mostly staying hung up and caught in the trees and brush.

Yet, at the end of the day, we would walk out with a string of fish (caught by Uncle Grady) and a good meal for that night's dinner table. I didn't realize at that time that he was teaching me one of the most important rules of fishing … especially smallmouth bass fishing … *Have Patience.*

It's really hard to explain just how important patience is in fishing. Let's think that. Just how important do you think patience is in your fishing? Multiply that by 10, and you have the answer.

Old Uncle Grady taught me a lot about that without me even knowing it. I'll never forget his effortless lessons on those precious backwaters of my youth.

As the days and years went by, my attention turned to the clear creeks near my home and all of the great fishing they had

My hero, Uncle Grady, 1962

Mr. Smallmouth's favorite meal

to offer. At first, my goal was to fill my stringer with whatever happened to be available. We fishermen like the tug of our line regardless of fish species. At the time, a good mess of fish on the dinner table was the best thing going, and still is in my book.

Then one day in the Harpeth River, something happened. As I tossed a live crawfish into a deep hole just below a piece of fast current, the water exploded with five pounds of smallmouth bass digging for the nearest cover. After a brief fight, (one I was not prepared for) the fish broke my line and was gone—never to be seen again, at least by my eyes. That was when I started to wonder why I hadn't caught this size fish before. I'd caught smallmouth bass before by the numbers, but they were all much smaller.

I then realized that **big** fish don't exist just anywhere in our lakes and streams. It sparked a saying I still use to this day: "There are big fish holes and little fish holes." From that moment on, my mind and heart were both hung up on Smallmouth bass.

As anglers, we've all found those fishing holes that produce fish, but most of these fish are small. Hopefully, we learn from our small fish mistakes and take it to the next level. If you really want to learn more about smallmouth bass, go to a clear creek and just watch. Spend some time on those calm, clear creeks and simply watch what swims by. If you're like me, you'll have a pole-in-hand in seconds, but taking time to watch will teach you a few lessons.

Here are a few things you'll observe:

1) Smallmouth bass will not live in direct current but they will run out in current to feed.

2) In moving water like a creek or river, smallmouth bass will live behind something ... be it a rock, log, stump or some other structure.

3) If there is no food in an area of the creek, then there will be no bass to catch. (Remember what we said earlier: a bass will never be too far from a food source.)

4) The big fish will be on or close to a mud/gravel/rocky bottom.

5) In creeks and rivers, a smallmouth bass will use wood cover more than any other structure on that body of water.

Once, many years ago, I was invited to fish the Squahana River in the northern part of the United States. It was an amazing river. It's two hundred yards wide in places, and yet there were very few places where you couldn't see the bottom. The water was crystal clear.

While I was there, I could envision a smallmouth bass on every rock and in each bend of the river. It was without doubt one of the most beautiful spots I'd ever been.

I set out in our bass boat with my fishing partner that day, navigating the twists and turns needed to avoid the shallow water rocks and snags scattered all over this scenic river. My son, Jay, was with me, too, manning the movie cameras to film some segments for my TV show.

As we raced up the river, Jay's eyes were trained on the clear bottom that looked very close to the hull of the boat. There were so many perfect smallmouth bass areas. As the day progressed, on either side of the river the beautiful shoreline was lined with the native trees of the area—some of which had fallen into the river. At that time, I had no idea the wooded cover would play such a large part in this trip.

As a smallmouth bass fisherman, I had my eye on the gravel and mud bottoms along with the ledges and large rocks. As the day progressed, we simply didn't catch as many fish as I thought we should, and strangely, the tree top cover was looking better all the time.

With that thought in mind, we eased the boat close to one of the treetops and made a cast to the outside edge. The water was clear enough that I saw the three pound smallmouth bass racing from his cover to inhale the 4″ slider worm. Jay and I both learned a valuable lesson that day … and we captured some good footage for the show.

Creeks and rivers are different from lakes in several ways. Perhaps the biggest factor is the amount of cover you find. Smallmouth bass like cover and structure, with structure being their best and first choice. Another thing to keep in mind is that smallmouth bass consider deeper water to be cover. This is a big one. Think on it.

In a current situation, bait placement is critical. Unlike the lake with no current, a bait can be kept in the same house for a long period of time—not in current, and that is why the presentation is so critical.

Most creeks and rivers have the same nearly-constant depth with the occasional deep-water area. As fisherman, we sometimes gravitate to these areas to find nothing ... and other times we can find a hole full of fish. If we find a hole full of fish, then other factors are probably present—a food source, possibly cover, and a place where the water is flowing into and out of the deep hole.

These conditions are prime areas for the fish to feed—food coming in, food trying to get out. Although smallmouth bass will not live in direct current, they will certainly take advantage of this current to feed before going back to the House. The mud and gravel bottoms still come into play just like in a lake, because crawfish live there.

When we approach these areas with our baits, we have to be looking for something in the way of cover for the fish. We can always make our casts into the deeper holes and catch fish, but the pattern for the day on the river or stream will be cover.

Creeks Were Made to Wade • 65

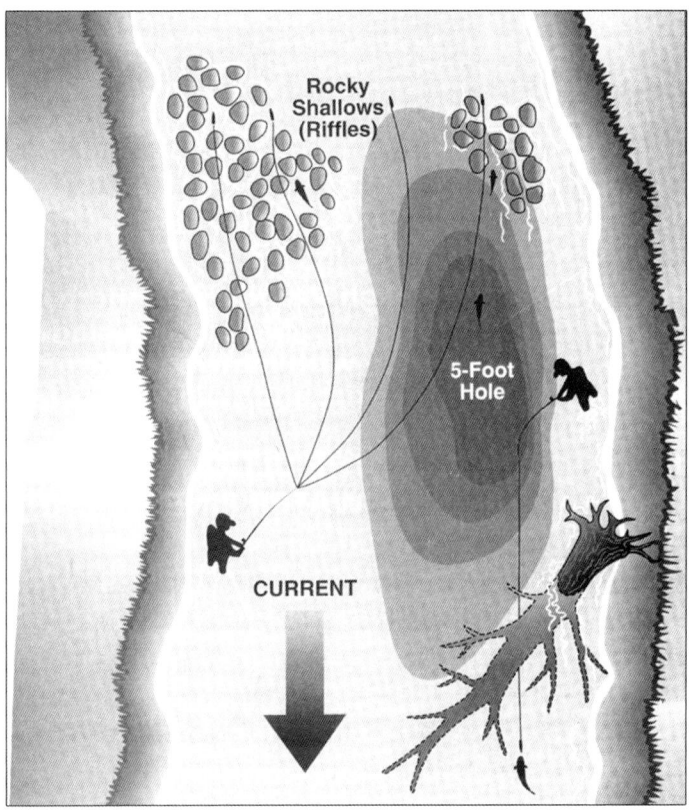

When fishing on foot, the best approach is to cast upstream so the lure or bait is worked downstream in natural fashion. Smaller, more active bass generally are found behind rocks in shallow water on the edge of heavy current. Larger bass like to hold behind rocks or in holes closer to shore. To fish a tree in the water, let the the lure or bait drift downstream into the structure from upstream. Illustrated by Lenny McPherson

We know that a smallmouth bass in current will live behind something that breaks the current flow. We also know that the bass will dart out into current to feed. These two things should tell us where to make our cast.

First, observe the way the current is breaking around the object (cover or structure). Watch the way the water swirls, and then try to make your cast so your bait follows that current line. This is a natural presentation to the fish. If you cast directly above the object you will probably get caught. If you cast directly behind the obstruction, your bait will move down current before the fish has a chance to strike. You might even spook the fish with your cast.

If the bait follows the natural current line enough times, you will probably entice the fish to strike. If you coax the fish away from the House and there are others there, you have a good chance at another fish as well. Remember ... in a creek there are less places that have cover, so more than one fish can and will occupy the same House (even our territorial Mr. Smallmouth). I believe they are just friendlier in a creek toward one another by necessity (particularly their own species). In places (like creeks) with few houses, the tenants stack up!

The Presentation

In a lake, the presentation can be in just about any direction if you are fishing deeper water. The current in creeks and rivers calls for something much different. When I am wading or boating in a current, I try to fish in an up-current situation. Upstream, I can make my casts as natural as possible. All of my casts will be ahead of the boat or at a forty-five degree angle to the boat. This presentation allows me to control my bait in a way that is more natural to what is happening around me. Once the bait gets even or at a ninety-degree angle to the boat, I reel it in and make another cast. The same casting action applies to wading—same casts, same retrieve. In the wading situation you have somewhat more control of the situation because of being able to stand in the same place for a longer period of time (you are not fighting to maintain boat position). Do not make a bad cast at a good spot without getting yourself in the best position. Being in a hurry is not the best thing to do. Remember what Uncle Grady taught me—*Patience*.

My son and favorite fishing partner, Jay, and a scrappy little river bronze-back.

What you learn in clear creeks is invaluable when fishing big water. You can see how the fish move, how they feed, and how they relate to cover and structure. You can also see how the fish behave in low and high-pressure.

In low pressure conditions, the area of influence increases, and the fish will roam further from the House. In high pressure conditions, you will find that the fish become more sluggish and will call for you to make a very close presentation with your bait. There really is no difference between the lake and the stream when it comes to barometric pressure and the way the fish react, so this is a great place to learn and actually see what's happening.

Learning to fish in current can help you to perfect your casting ability, because your casts must be so precise in those conditions. Choices of baits become important in the creeks, also, because you can watch a fish just swim away from something she doesn't like and try to rip apart something that she finds appealing. You can learn all of this fishing in a creek, plus you get the added bonus of being able to see what you're fishing for and learn from the visuals you witness.

I carried my son, Jay, to the creeks on my shoulders when he was small, and he learned many important facts about fish and fishing in these small pristine pools of water—just like I did. It's something we both remember and hold dear in our hearts.

I wish that I could write thirty more pages on the subjects of creeks, rivers and moving water, but I don't need to. The simple fact is once you get back to those four things we discussed earlier ... the *House* to live in, a *Bottom Conducive to the Fish*, *Access to Deep Water*, and a food source coupled with *Presentation*, you have 80 percent of the puzzle solved.

Are there different baits and altered presentations to be made? Of course ... but those are up to you. The bottom line is this: you can learn as much or more sitting on a high creek bank watching what is happening in the water for two days than you can in a year of haphazard fishing on a lake in ten trips. The old expression still applies: *Watch and Learn.*

Baits

While creeks and rivers often call for lots of the same baits you would use in a lake situation, there are some that are better than others. While I'm a grub fanatic (self-proclaimed and proven!), I don't often use jigs and grub baits in creeks, and seldom use them in rivers. I would much rather have a bottom-working bait like an artificial crawfish or 4" worm when in a river condition—like a slider worm fished on a lead head. Most all of the fish in a creek are going to be caught feeding on the bottom, so that's where I want my bait to be 90 percent of the time. The same holds true for rivers, but you can add the top water bait in those situations.

Now ... for the biggest reason to take those trips to a clear creek. It's just plain fun! There have been too many times when I've been on the water and seen a father and son in their boat and the son is sitting in the back just throwing because

These two boys are plucking crawfish from the seine, placing them in their bait bucket.

he has no idea what he's doing. He simply has not had the opportunity to learn.

The father is doing a wonderful thing by taking his son or daughter fishing. We need more of that in our new-fangled world. Kids have a need to learn. Go with them to a clear creek and take a box of worms or a bucket of crawfish, maybe even some artificial bait, and let them see what's going in the water. Then let them see how old dad approaches a good fishing hole. Let them fish and watch their excitement as they learn the things needed to make them the best fishing partners you'll ever have.

Uncle Grady and me — March 1958

Jay ... doing what he does best.

Take the time ... and when they hang into that five-pound smallmouth and you go into the dock to show it off ... that young man or young lady will turn to someone and say, "My Dad taught me to do that." You will never hear better words. My Uncle Grady taught me to do that. It's one of my greatest and fondest memories.

Take the kids to the river and show them a thing or two. It's priceless.

CHAPTER NINE

Colors

When I was starting out in the smallmouth bass fishing business, I was often asked if bait color made any difference. My answer to this is without a doubt, yes. Even though bass cannot tell yellow from red in our sense of understanding, Smallmouth might sense those subtle shades better than most. They are much smarter than most other fish, and they can tell shades of color depending on their environment. By this, I mean the color of the water or the clouds in the sky.

When judging color, there have always been norms to go by. Clear water, clear bait—dark water, dark bait. There are exceptions to every rule, and these norms have been broken thousands of times by fisherman around the world. It happens, but not on a consistent basis. It's just not in the cards.

Fish react to color by what they think the bait represents. The fish think it's a shad or a crawfish, so the colors we use also depend on the way we are presenting it to the fish.

I choose color in several ways. I carefully evaluate the clarity of the water, how sunny or cloudy it is, and what color the bottom is.

If you're keeping up, I'll bet you thought I was going to say the color of the bait fish or crawfish on the bottom was a factor. If I was largemouth bass fishing, I'd probably try to match the color of my bait in some way to the color of the prey, but not when fishing for smallmouth. Keep in mind that right now we're strictly focusing on smallmouth bass.

A quick story

Years ago, I designed a grub for a bait company based in Florida. We played with the shape and size of the bait until we had what we wanted, and then we discussed colors. After settling on ten color options, I hopped a plane and headed back to Tennessee for some much needed rest (on the water of course).

Sometime later, I received the first grubs. I was greatly disappointed when I opened the package and saw the coloration of my first batch. Green. They were, ugly, ugly green.

I picked up the phone and demanded, "What is this junk color?"

"We were cleaning out the molding machine and this color just happened to be in the hopper," they told me. "Just try them, not for the color, but for the action of the grub."

I had about a hundred of the grubs, so I passed out a few to some of my fishing buddies and we headed to the lake. It was late April, and the grub bite was on.

A few hours later, one of my buddies came back to my marina and said the magic words. *You got any more of those grubs?*

After a brief conversation, I jumped in the boat with him, and we headed out. I put on my favorite amber pepper grub, and he used the ugly, ugly green one.

I can tell you for a fact that it doesn't take me long to recognize a hot light bulb moment. That day, the green was deadly, and one fish after another was coming to the boat. I was catching some on the amber pepper, but the ugly green was out-pacing me three to one.

What was even more surprising was we were catching all kinds of fish—bass, crappie, hybrids—whatever saw the green grub, ate it. It was simply wonderful.

We'll come back to this story shortly, once we cover a few more thoughts on coloration and transparency of our baits.

As I said earlier, picking colors has some *so called* rules of thumb. I like clear or semi-transparent grubs in clear water. If the sun is shining bright, I also like to have some glitter in the grub. If it gets cloudy, I may use the same grub but without the glitter.

Example

Clear water, bright sun—transparent chartreuse grub with silver glitter.

Clear water, cloudy conditions—transparent chartreuse grub, no glitter. (I may choose to go with an amber pepper coloration here, too. I'll tell you why in later pages.)

One of my all-time favorite colors …
Amber Pepper

Why would I change to the amber pepper? Amber pepper is not a solid color. Fish hit a bait for what they think the bait represents. If I am swimming a grub through the water, it's a minnow to the fish. If the bait is on the bottom, it's a crawfish. It's that simple.

If that same crawfish looking grub in amber pepper comes swimming just off the bottom, the fish are more likely to believe it might be a crawfish. If so, he'll test it out—see if it really is a crawfish. The only way he can test it is to taste it. Bingo! Set the hook.

We humans do the same thing in our lives if you think about it. Have you ever gone into a grocery store and bought tomatoes without feeling a few of them first? It's just a natural thing to do. Fish react much the same way we do. He'll test that bait a little if he's wary. That is precisely why *feel* is so important when fishing grubs of any color. It only takes him a second to spit that thing out if it doesn't seem natural.

On those aggressive days when bass gulp anything that moves, it might be a different story. But Mr. Smallmouth isn't dumb. He'll test it to see if it's *really* a crawfish. Don't give him time to decide it isn't.

Having mentioned all of this, I want to get back to the ugly green grub story. After fishing the green grub for a few days and catching smallmouth bass like you would not believe, suddenly that ugly green color was getting much prettier to me! A few days later, I took the lady I'd been dating out on the lake. I'd been gone a lot on the road, so our *together time* was important to us both. And ... I wanted her to catch some fish 'cause I needed some extra credit points with her for being gone all the time!

I'm sure she would have preferred to go shopping ... or at the very least, move some of the fishing tackle around so she could sunbathe without fear of an accidental hook-set.

Arizona is a beautiful place, and I have been there many times. Lake Apache is just 40 miles outside of Phoenix and is one of four lakes on the Salt River. Those pristine waters are just full of smallmouth.

The water had a green tint to it on this day, because the algae bloom was coming on. After she'd taken some good fish, I asked her, "How do you like that grub color?"

Her answer to my simple question has stuck with me for a long time. She said, "It should catch fish if it looks like everything down there." Truer words were never spoken—and a new chapter in smallmouth bass fishing was coming into my head.

To carry this simple, yet milestone story even further, I'd like to make another point. During that December, I had a tournament to fish in Arizona. It was a Smallmouth-only tournament. I had a collection of green grubs that no one had ever seen in my tackle box for the day. I felt like the tournament was in the bag.

Practice day came around, and I eased away from the dock. When I arrived at my first spot, I tied on the green grub and made a cast—then another ... and another ... and many, many more without a single bite.

What is wrong with this picture? I kept asking myself that same question. Then, I tied on the amber pepper grub and at the next hole I caught a smallmouth.

Okay ... I thought I'd found the fish—so back to the green grub I went. Again, no fish. Back to the amber pepper—another bass came to the boat.

Then ... A flash of brilliance hit me! (You know us fisherman don't have many flashes!)

What that little lady said months ago came back to me—*It looks like everything down there.*

Everything on the bottom of that lake was *brown* ... the rocks, the sand, even the flooded-over cactus that have been in the lake for years. The green color was out of the ordinary in this reservoir. My "Great Green Grub" that worked so well 1,600 miles away in Percy Priest Lake just didn't cut it on these different bottom conditions.

I was in Arizona on Lake Apache ... nothing down there looked like my ugly green specialty grub. The only algae bloom and plant growth here was in the aquarium at the marina. Rock, sand, gravel, boulders—all brown. The green grub just did not fit in here.

The point of this long-winded story is that color makes a difference at the right time, in the right spot, under the right weather conditions. This is true whether it be a grub, a tube jig, or a lead-head hair fly.

I'm going to give you a list my favorite colors for grubs, tubes, and hair flies. Most are alike with a few subtle differences.

Grub

Chartreuse, chartreuse with silver glitter, clear amber pepper, Green (Two shades light and dark), clear smoke (silver glitter), Gold (Gold glitter).

Arizona's wonderful water

Tube:

Clear amber pepper, amber pepper with black-flake, clear-silver with silver glitter, black, black with red flake.

Fly:

Brown, black, brown and orange, white, chartreuse

> **NOTE:** *The only world record smallmouth bass ever caught on eight-pound test line was hooked on a smoke-glitter grub in Dale Hollow Lake in the spring of 1986. Mr. Paul Beal of Indiana caught his 10 pound, 8 ounce beauty mid-lake by simply dragging his smoke-colored grub on those muddy flats. His fish is the third largest on the overall World Record Chart.*

Paul Beal and his eight-pound test line World Record 10 lb. 8 ounce 1986 (Third Largest Overall)

Are there other colors that will catch fish? Of course there are. I have fished all over the U.S. and a few other countries with these colors ... and very seldom do they let me down. If I'm in the boat with someone, and he's catching fish on another color—will I change to that color? You bet your sweet bippy I will. I'm persistent, but not stubborn enough to be unwilling to change. It isn't about who's right ... it's about catching fish.

I've caught countless fish on other color varieties, but by-and-large, the colors I listed are my mainstays. I like them. I've tested them. I've had great success with them. I try to stay consistent when possible, while still keeping an open mind. It's very easy to go color crazy by trying to have them all. So don't take that path, there are just too many colors out there.

The colors *you* ultimately choose may be slightly different from mine, and that's fine and to be expected. Yet I'll bet that after you try them all, you'll end up with five color combos that you catch 90 percent of your fish on.

Earlier we talked about the Zara Spook as my best top water bait. I love it. I own about twenty of them—and about 15 of them are blue-backed and chrome-sided. Ninety percent of the bass I've caught on that bait have been on blue and chrome. It's a color a smallmouth bass just can't seem to resist in clear water.

Keep in mind that most of the colors I'm telling you about relate to the soft plastics, and not necessarily to crank bait or spinner bait. These are primarily grub and jig colors that have proven their catching power for me. What I am giving you is a reflection of the baits I've experimented with for years that work for me ... and I know they will work for you, too.

By testing these color options on a regular basis *and* documenting the results, your chance of success and your general knowledge of smallmouth color preferences will increase greatly.

Another story on color

People send me new baits all the time, and I like that. It allows me to test new ideas and stay sharp and on my game.

Once, many years ago, I was in the boat with Jay having a good day on the water. Someone had sent me a pathetic pink top-water bait. It was gawd-awful ugly, but I had it in the boat that day, nonetheless.

Jay, who was 15 at the time, reached for the bait to give it a try.
Waste of time, Son. Don't bother.

Later, he reached again for that same ugly bubblegum-looking thing lying unwanted in the bottom of the boat.
Waste of time, Son. Don't bother.

After his third attempt to tie on that lure, I relinquished … and tied it on.

One cast—and one eight-pound largemouth later—his words ground into my pride …

"You told me, Dad, *try different things …*"

I seriously have to watch what I say around that boy. I guess that even this old dog learns a new trick now and then.

So the main gist of this chapter is simple:

- Trust your records.
- Study the color patterns above by witnessing your surroundings and making adjustments accordingly.
- Document and learn.

Start with tried and true color patterns and build your new "color" arsenal through practice, patience, and by trying a little-something-new now and then … even if it's an ugly green, or gawd-awful pink one your annoyingly-persistent son likes …

Note the slightly different color patterns of the two fish.

"Real milestones in an angler's life are measured only between man and fish ... and that fine line that comes between us."

*~ **Darren Shell***

The Old Thompson Doll Fly, possibly the best selling lure of all time

CHAPTER TEN

The Hair Fly

The lead head hair fly has been a mainstay in my smallmouth bass arsenal for as long as I've been a smallmouth bass fisherman. The hair fly and smallmouth bass go together like peaches and cream. Its versatility is unmatched and its fish-catching profile is at the top of the list. There may be baits as good but it's a mistake if you don't include this piece of fishing dynamite in your arsenal.

Which came first ... the chicken or the egg? It might as well be *Which came first ... the tackle box or the fly?*

As the lakes start to warm after a long winter of blustery weather, few baits will attract fish like the fly. It's simplicity and effectiveness will forever guarantee its place in America's tackle box. The grub is hard to beat, but until the water starts to warm into the high 50s, the fly is by-far the superior bait. Its action is not affected by the cold water like plastic is—and the number of trailers a fisherman can use with it are unlimited.

I have to refer to my Uncle Grady again to tell you about my first experience with a fly. I remember the crudely-molded ones he made and used. They were quite rough by today's standards in comparison to the finely-polished, machine-made varieties that now fill the tackle aisles of the outdoor shops. His were all-white as best as I can remember, and probably a quarter ounce in size with a big hook. Even the hook wasn't made to be molded into a jig head. It was just a hook squeezed into some lead, but those antiquated old jigs sure did catch the fish!

Those less-than-perfect old hand-tied flies caught everything from crappy to bluegill—walleye to stripe—and yes ... even Smallmouth bass.

Let's talk about the trailer. A little something dangling off the back of your hook is a good thing—it's enticing to the fish. As a kid, I watched Uncle Grady take a box of worms and catch bluegill. He'd scale the bluegill and cut long thin strips of the meat and skin and attach those strips to the back of the fly. He'd fish

John Gorman and his 2nd World Record Smallmouth 10 pound 14 ounce. Taken on a white Doll Fly in 1969. Also pictured, Lloyd Harrison, Sunset Marina owner. Dale Hollow Lake, Tennessee

that fly in a swimming motion through the water, mimicking a darting minnow.

I think the people who used this bait felt that the meat on the back of the hook caught the fish, and that the fly was just a weighted and controllable way to get it to them. In all actuality, it was a combination of both. Those natural meaty trailers enticed fish with something that *looked like what was down there* (remember my lady-friend's words?). It worked.

Uncle Grady's crude old flies will forever be in my memory. Good fishing is good for making good memories.

It wasn't many years later that the hair fly became a mainstay in my tackle box. I was swimming the fly on Woods Reservoir when I was 10 years old—and that was a long time ago. For over 25 years, I've conducted seminars across the country using the swimming fly technique as a big part of my talks, but it was at a boat show in Nashville, Tennessee, that I gave my first talk about swimming the fly.

Here comes another story …

I remember the first seminar I ever gave—that special day in Nashville in 1981. Harry Renfro, a show promoter, brought an outdoor show to Nashville and held it at the fairgrounds. There were tons of booths and exhibits scattered through the buildings and parking lots of south Nashville's fairground facility. I had my first fishing guide booth set up at that show, and was booking fishing trips at the rate of (are you ready for this?) $60.00 per day. *Wow, have times changed!*

Harry hadn't booked any speakers that day for entertainment. He'd had trouble with scheduling or something, and was in a bit of a bind. He came by my booth and asked me if I'd like to give a short seminar. I let him know that I'd never done one before and really didn't know what to talk about.

"What do you like best, fishing-wise?" he asked.
"Smallmouth bass," I replied.
"Okay ... do that."

I was beyond skeptical about jumping out in front of thousands of people and rambling about my fishing techniques ... especially for the first time. But I gotta tell ya, Harry's next words shook me.

"Do you want to stand in that booth the rest of your life? Get out there and make something of yourself."

Needless to say, I did the talk, and my ramblings have continued since that day. You wanna know what I talked about that special day in my life—surrounded by great fishermen and enthusiasts of all varieties, while all eyes were on little old me? I talked about swimming a fly.

Simple as that. The old mainstay hair fly began my lecturing career. Uncle Grady had somehow come to my rescue once again! It was another fond fishing memory and something that has touched many people.

After that, as fate would have it, I began giving seminars all over the country. Soon thereafter, I decided that fishing was what I wanted to do as my life work. I did seminars at the Indianapolis Boat Sport and Travel Show for Dan Renfro, Harry's son, which fueled the fires for many more to come.

Over the next twenty-five years, I averaged over 60 days a year giving talks from California to Maine, Alabama to Canada, Nova Scotia, and even a couple of foreign countries that I can't pronounce. I really felt blessed to be able to do what I love and share my fishing knowledge with people around the globe.

It was both wonderful and humbling to give those talks around the world and see the reactions of the audiences to little old me. You know what? That old stand-by *swimming the fly* method was in every speech I gave. All of them. It hit home and stuck there. (Or should I say hit-House?)

A Hawg of a Smallmouth

I found it easy to convince people about the grub and top water bait, but the fly was just a little harder, especially in the northern states where the fly techniques had not caught on. Even where they had entered the fishing realm, most fishermen would never use them for smallmouth bass.

Some did take the old fly by the horns and use it successfully in their native waters. It took some talking on my part, but today, it's catching on more and more.

Everyone likes to be a part of something in life, and I hope that people will remember me for the fly and grub techniques I've preached for all these many years. That old fly and old Uncle Grady have shaped my life.

***

How do we fish the hair fly? If you look back at the chapter on fishing the grub and substitute fly everywhere you see grub, you'll understand part of it. Including the slow and steady retrieve—just off of the bottom, the countdown method over deep water, and the same fishing places. Yet there is so much more to the fly than those techniques alone.

The fly is one of the most versatile baits the smallmouth bass fisherman can load on the end of his line. (Notice I said *load* on your line. It's a heavy-duty firearm for smallmouth). Here's how we successfully present this simple bait to the fish.

The fly, unlike the grub, requires a trailer—and the number of trailers is nearly unlimited. Pork and plastic make up the bulk of trailers that can be used with the fly.

The fly can be fished on the bottom, or just off of the bottom—or both—on the same cast. It can be fished slow or fast depending on the fish—shallow or deep in the mud or over the rocks. Anywhere.

Important fact:

In the hot part of the summertime when the grub fishing starts to slow ... the fly is hitting its peak. What I'm trying to say is that there is no time of the year that the fly won't catch fish if you can get it to the water. It's a timeless wonder.

As I stated earlier, there are countless trailers for your fly. During my seminars, I've talked about a fisherman wanting to have more baits than his neighbor. It's kind of one of those "He who dies with the most toys" type of things ... I must confess, I'm the same way, but with flies and trailers.

This may be a little hard to follow, but you should get a laugh out of it as well as a new outlook on fishing the fly.

As all-knowing and caveman-like manly men, and collectors of colors and sizes and shapes of all baits known to man, we all want a lot of baits in all the "purdy" colors. And that's okay. It might even be the ugly pink ones Jay likes ... We like to organize them in cool plastic boxes and show them off to the neighbors.

Look at the list below. How many collective baits are there? Now think hard. If you said 36 ... you missed it by 84. There are over a hundred different combinations there to be tried. Will you use all of the combinations? Probably not. Will you use 20? Without question. You'll find your favorites and slap the waters with them.

- Lets take four fly colors in three sizes 1/8, 3/16, 1/14 — total 12 baits
- Now, lets add four colors each of 3″ and 4″ grubs — total 8 baits
- Two different sizes of Uncle Josh U-2 and U-3 in 4 colors — total 8 baits
- Two different sizes of Uncle Josh 101 and 11, 4 colors — total 8 baits

Example:

If we put a black grub on a black fly, that's one. If we put four different color grubs on the same fly, that's four baits. If we put four different color grubs of two sizes on the same fly, we have eight different baits. The combinations are mind-boggling. Add pork rinds into the mix, and you have plenty to stock your fly arsenal.

As I list my favorite colors of flies and trailers, you will find what seems like a contradiction. I said that I like the transparent colors in grubs in clear waters—I think they are much better at catching smallmouth bass than solid colors (given grub fishing conditions). Yet, here with the fly, we are fishing it in the same conditions using all solid colors.

Why do they work? That's a tough question. I hate to say this, but I'm not exactly sure why they work. I just know they do.

If you look at the differences, you'll probably notice the profile in the water and the action—especially the action. If I'm crawling a fly and grub on the bottom, it's still a crawfish to the bass. If I'm swimming it through the water, it'll be a shad or bait fish to the bass. If I hop it up and down on the bottom, the bass think it's a fly hopping up and down on the bottom ... but they eat it anyway.

Favorite colors

- Hair fly — black, brown, chartreuse, white
- Grub (2) sizes 3″ & 4″ — black, amber pepper, white, chartreuse

Combinations: In either pork or fly applications.

- Black and brown combinations
- White and chartreuse combinations

I sometimes use purple when casting the bigger pork chunks on my black or brown fly. It seems to give it a little extra *something* to entice the fish. The fly will by far give you many hours of enjoyment on the water and help you put lots of fish in the boat.

Many times I've met my fishing partners at the lake for a day or night of fishing, simply carrying a brown paper bag filled with flies, pork, and grubs. It's called a "Tennessee Tackle Box"… and I own several. In my last book, I mentioned *The World's Smallest Tackle Box*. This is it. I'd hate to toss out that Zara Spook or perfect Rapala, but this baby is the simplest fish producer you can buy.

Keep in mind that every time you change the trailer on these flies, you make a new bait … *to the fish*. Those subtle differences each day on the lake make much more sense to the fish than perhaps to you, the fisherman. But be persistent in your color options … study, document, and catch fish. It'll happen in that order.

Whether you cast the new-age type of perfect flies, or create your own type of Uncle Grady-style hand-made fly kit … know that this antiquated old mainstay, the fly bait, is a mainstay for a reason—it works.

Thanks, Uncle Grady. In my heart and soul, you've changed my fishing career with your neat old flies … and more importantly, you've changed my early days with your heart-felt life lessons taught to a little boy wading the rivers of middle Tennessee. ~Tony

Darren Shell holding his first Float-N-Fly Smallie

A Note from Darren on the Float-N-Fly

Tony asked me to share some cold water Dale Hollow Float-N-Fly knowledge with you. This technique has become a real mainstay for fishermen on the deeper and clearer lakes in the mid-south. Although this book isn't intended to focus on any particular region of the world, we'd still like to share this strange and fairly new amendment to our fishing methods.

This is not one of Tony's favorite forms of fly fishing, but he wanted it included within his book, because it's a method that will no-doubt continue to be used for years to come. It requires special gear and special tackle to implement, but the results are definitely worth the challenge of learning the craft.

The controversy over where this art started spans a decade. Most of the guides and practitioners of this type of fishing believe (adamantly) that it was started in east Tennessee by a small group of crappie fishermen who were disgusted with all the smallmouth "wasting" their time on their bobber rigs. "We can't catch crappie for all those darned smallmouths wastin' our time."

Nice problem to have, huh?

Well, this system is exactly what it sounds like … a floating fly. I'm not going to get into great detail about this type of rig because there are many great articles and videos about it online for those who want to investigate it in depth. I do, however, want to explain why this system is used and what its attributes are. In a nut shell, this is how the system is rigged and why.

During the cold and blustery months of winter, smallmouth metabolism slows immensely. Getting these fish to be aggressive is nearly impossible. Most are suspended on or near a sharp bluff wall. Trying to swim a grub or fly through the water slow enough for them at this time of year is problematic. It just slides on by too quickly for the bass to care. So how can we slow it down? The savvy crappie fishermen figured it out for us by accident.

A long monofilament leader made of four pound test between 12′ to 15′ long is attached to a three-way swivel with a bobber on one end. A very small jig (usually 1/16-oz.) is tied to the other end of the leader, creating a long jig-and-bobber leader combo. Since sliding bobbers just don't seem to function all that well with small jigs, this leader system is used. There just isn't enough weight to tug the line through the slip-bobber, so the fisherman must now determine how he'll throw this long and gangly contraption of 15′ of line.

A very long pole like the old standard fly-rods is used to "whip" this float and fly up near the bluff wall. Once that jig sinks to its leader's length, the bobber stands up and the jig suspends, lightly jigging itself with the tiny wave actions on the lake surface above.

What we have is a suspended jig for a suspended fish. Part of the fun of this system is that you can throw it a mile. Cast it up next to shore and fish it like a standard fly. Once it hits its depth, slow down and let the bobber do the work. A little tug toward the boat now and then is all it takes.

The real beauty of this form of fishing is that once the angler learns to cast this contraption (with practice), it provides several necessary things for cold, clear water fishing:

- Allows extremely light line to be cast into the wind.
- Allows nearly invisibly light line to be used in the crystal water.
- Allows very slow fishing when fish are not particularly active.
- It doesn't take a rocket scientist to know when you've got a bite. When that cork goes under—set the hook and reel him in.
- Plus, this method almost ALWAYS hooks the fish in the upper lip. Rarely does a fish swallow this fly, possibly jeopardizing its life.

The system isn't designed for every lake or stream, but some deeper, clear water lakes are prime targets for this way of swimming a fly. Look it up online. It's a blast to learn and even more fun once you get the hang of it. There's just something about watching a cork going under… ~ DS

CHAPTER ELEVEN

Smallmouth Can Be Spoon-fed

We've talked substantially about our grubs, flies, and top water baits, but one more great fishing lure has been left in the shadows. I'd like to discuss the simplistic, but powerful jigging spoon.

There are times when the Smallmouths are just not playing along with our game. Sometimes, and I hate to say it, those golden beauties just don't quite cooperate with my tried and true methods and my strategy of throwing flies and grubs. In those certain times, I like to think of my Smallmouth prey as a little kid with an attitude.

Ever see a child that's plainly not hungry and certainly not interested in what you want him to eat? Smallmouths are often in that same category. Sometimes you must entice those temperamental kids to eat, somehow—some way. Some days, those finicky smallmouth creatures just don't want the usual and common modes of bait trickery. On days like these, I turn to another old stand-by—the spoon. We can "spoon"-feed those scrappy little bass and get them to eat.

Let me share another little story *(I do love stories.)*

Years back, a friend of mine, Conrad Jones, was fishing with me at a Smallmouth Bass Team Club Tournament on Percy Priest Lake. We needed two more Smallmouth to fill our tournament limit of 5 bass ... and time was waning. As we fished on one of our favorite spots, a mud flat in 10´ of water, we kept seeing a big fish busting shad top water some distance from the boat. (Have you ever noticed that when you see these fish they're always about 20´ further away than anything you can cast?)

This was one of those times. I watched these fish for many minutes until I cracked. Finally, I couldn't stand it any longer and reached down into my tackle box and came out with a ¾ oz. Critter Gitter spoon. I tied it on a spinning reel with 8-pound test line and set it aside for that next jump I was sure was going to happen.

BOMBER SLAB SPOON

Note the bouncing spoon on the graph section and the immediate fish strike to the right of it!

Sure enough, the next time the fish came up, I picked up the rod and gave a cast right at the swirl. This heavy type of bait can be cast at great length—much farther than our flies and grubs.

When the spoon hit at the swirl and sank just for a second, the line jerked snug, and I set the hook. There was so much bag in my line from the long cast, that I had to run to the back of the boat to help get all the stretch out of the line. I nearly knocked ol' Conrad off the back of the boat, but that was okay—he shouldn't have been in my way! This is important bass fishing!

After a lengthy fight, a 6 lb., 4 oz. smallmouth bass came to the boat. I know the weight precisely because it was the big bass of the day—and I looked it up in my records just be sure. We won that tournament and got first and second big fish. Without the spoon-fed bass, it would have been third place and the big bass of the day would have been Conrad's 5 lb., 9 oz. beauty.

The spoon won us some money that day and has helped create special days for me in the years since. It's almost like a secret weapon lying in the floor of your boat. When opportunity knocks … grab that thing and give it a whirl. It's like that Zara Spook lying next to it, both are very important tools to use in unison with whatever bait I'm throwing every time I go out.

When those guys at the dock ask what I caught 'em on … I can just point to the rods in my boat. "Caught 'em all on those poles." Let them do the math.

Sometimes you just have to break from the norm and do something different. I never go out now without a spoon tied on one rod and reel. I may not use it all day long, but it's there if I need it.

***

The spoon came into play again for me in a tournament in Arizona. It was one of those blue bird days with no wave action caused by the wind on the water. It was just a dead day on the lake ... one of those perfectly sunny, high-pressure ones we talked about earlier.

I hate to admit it, but all of my old standby baits just weren't working. I had to do something out of the norm. As I motored around watching my graph, I noticed fish stacked on the deep drops at the end of points at about 22´ deep. I counted-down the grub and the hair fly to the right depth to no avail. I felt that I was just not keeping the bait in the fish's area long enough. Sometimes, keeping a fly at a certain depth may still be a little too fast to suit the bass.

While pondering my dilemma, a flash of brilliance hit me (that's two flashes I've had in this book—not bad for a southern Smallmouth bass fisherman). I tied on a ¾ once spoon and counted it down to the exact depth and started the yo-yo bump as I call it (I will explain in just a minute). A fish took the spoon, and when it came to the surface I could see the browns of the smallmouth shining in the clear water.

I took my tournament on that spot in a matter or minutes. I caught 5 fish in five drops of the spoon in that same small area on the point. While I came in second in the tournament, another valuable lesson in smallmouth bass fishing would be placed in my inky records. The spoon became another tool in my successful smallmouth bass fishing.

***

One method to fish the spoon is to wait for the fish to come up in those sporadic jumps and cast. But the more precise method of counting-down that bait is the one you need to file away in your memory banks.

Fish that are suspended on the sides of drops in large schools often are not feeding and have to be provoked or prodded into striking any sort of bait. It's sort of like if you've just eaten dinner, and you're just sitting there on the couch with your belt let out swearing that you will never eat again for the rest of your life, then someone walks into the room and starts eating a big piece of cheese cake right in front of you. The urge to get up and cut you a slab of desert is sometimes overwhelming. That's what we want the fish to feel like when the spoon is dancing in front of their faces for a long period of time. The only way to do that is to know exactly where the bait is at all times … hence the countdown.

Here's how I accomplish it. This method will be done fishing directly down beneath the boat. This isn't a casting type of fishing. This is a controlled vertical tactic. Although we count down our flies and grubs after a cast, this is a line-length counting procedure.

First, you need to know the distance from the spool of the reel you're using to the first eye of the rod (in this method it's probably a bait caster). This first eye is called the stripper guide. Let's say, for this example, the distance is 24″. Also for this example, let's say the fish are in 20′ to 24′ of water.

With the rod at a 90° angle from waist-high (straight out from your belt-line), pull line from the reel to the striper guide, either using the drag feature on the reel or by slowly spooling off the proper length of line. One pull equals 2′ of let-out line. Ten pulls equals 20′, etc.

After these precise calculations, you know that you're at the top of the school of fish you found on the graph.

Now, lower the rod tip to just off the top of the water, make three short sharp jerks to get back to waist high and allow the line to tighten and drop the spoon back down again.

> **NOTE:** *Always drop the rod down with a tight line—90 percent of the strikes will occur on the fall. Be ready for that hit on the drop.*

There have been few times that I've had to try different colors of spoons to form my patterns. Size doesn't seem to make much difference either. I like a ¾ ounce size 99 percent of the time. My usual choice of colors is blue or black with chrome sides or green with white sides. All of these colors will have a treble hook with a white buck tail. The treble hooks that most spoons come with will be okay. With the techniques I've described, a straight and solid spoon will work best.

As I've already said, the spoon is not one of those baits that you'll start the day with, but it is one that will put fish in the live well for you.

Conrad and I sure enjoyed many days tossing those spoons out on the lake. Sadly, we lost him in 2010 after a long illness. He was my fishing partner, but most of all, he was a good friend. We shared many wonderful moments on the water together. He was a smallmouth bass enthusiast like me who believed that time on the water with a fishing rod in your hand should be experienced by everyone at least once. I will miss my old friend, and I will never forget our fun fishing times chasing smallmouth bass.

My buddy and fishing partner, Conrad Jones

*Remember, days you don't go
to the water are just another day.
Days spent on the water are always special.
Take a friend and make some memories.*

~Tony Bean

CHAPTER TWELVE

Keeping Records

We have touched on keeping records throughout this book. It does not make any difference if you fish ten times a year or fifty, records are *to me*, a must. I know I'll be back the next year and odds are it'll be at the same time of the year within a few days. Just a quick glance back at my records will tell me a lot about the upcoming trip.

It might seem a bit overboard, but there are times when I Velcro a tape recorder to the windshield of my boat. I'll record a few bits of interesting data as I fish. It goes back to those rabbits and wildlife. I try to document those types of things as well. Maybe there was a huge die-off of shad that week. Maybe I noticed more loons working the waters. Many things tie-in to catching fish. It doesn't hurt to jot them all down or tape record them and log them into your record system when you get the time.

I have a certain system I use and the information I gather is incorporated into that system. It's fun going back through years of carefully saved data and checking all the facts you've recorded. You might be surprised at just how close your next fishing trip will be to one on a previous year. If the water temps are close, and the water table is similar to a year you've documented, you may just have similar results.

This is good in many ways. For instance, it might be that you caught many fish last year and want to return on a similar day. Perhaps more important is the fact that you can only slip away from work or obligations one day this week … you'll want to make the best of your day on the water. Pick a day that your records show to be best. Then, find a way to take two days off! Remember, days you don't go to the water are just another day. Days spent on the water are always special. Take a friend and make some memories.

Another good addition to your records is a film archive. Take your camera along with you to the lake. Take videos or still pictures of what you see, what you do … everything. Write down the spot on paper and hold it in front of the camera and take a picture so you have the information documented. This will give you instant information about the spot when you review later. Digital photography and video is so easy to transfer this day and age that it should become one of your smallmouth bass fishing tools.

If you happen to live on a lake that has a winter draw-down period, this is the prime time to check lots of different areas. While you're making your survey, keep in mind three of the four factors we've discussed: *the House, Bottom Conducive to the Fish, and Access to Deep Water.* While lakes that are drawn-down will not uncover the deepest water haunts of the smallmouth, they will uncover the flats the smallmouth bass will use during the spawning period where they spend the pre- and post-spawn cycles of their lives. You don't have to mark every small piece of cover on those flats, but definitely pick the ones that seem out of the ordinary.

Richard Craig and a pretty four- pounder

Example:

You pull up on a flat and there's nothing *different* on any part of the flat. This is probably not the best spot to mark. However, you pull up on the next flat and there's an old stump row leading into deep water. This could've been an old fence row or the edge of a wood line where hard wood turned to soft, and the soft wood is now long gone. There may be a part of an old house or barn foundation nearby or even a roadbed. As the water rises over this old road bed, it will again be a highway for smallmouth bass. The same applies to the stump row.

Also look for transitions in the bottom structure: gravel to rock, rock to mud, and so on. These edges will always be places where fish travel and feed. Mark them down, GPS them, take photos. Document it all, and put this new information in your system.

Let's say you find a flat that has none of the features mentioned above but it does have a ditch leading from the bank to deeper water. This small depth change is all you may need to have a great day on the water.

Smallmouth bass like something that is irregular in nature. Now this may sound funny, but let's say I pulled up on a flat with the water down, and there were ten stumps that will be in 4´ of water when the water rises again. On that same spot I can see two large stumps sticking just out of the water and they'll be in 8´ of water when the water rises. I'll mark the ten stumps, but I'll make every effort to make sure I can get back to the two stumps that are in deeper water. You will not catch a ton of fish here, but you will take that big fish. The perfect House will always be occupied by the big boys on the block. If Big Boy moves out … someone else will move in.

How do we find these spots again after the water comes back up? We talked about a few pictures and video. But how do we get on the exact spot when our first cast hits in the House? A GPS is definitely the best and easiest system, but not everyone owns one of those expensive digital toys. If there's no GPS, we can use a method called *cross-triangulation* (big word for this old guide!)

Another little story

I'd written an article for *Infisherman* magazine called "X Marks the Spot". It dealt with just what we've been talking about. Soon after the article was published, Larry Dalbuerg, one of the editors and a cameraman came to Percy Priest Lake to do a show. As we pulled across the lake and fished different spots, we finally came to the spot I'd used to illustrate my story.

As we got closer, one of the guys looked ahead and said, "This is the spot you drew in the book." Larry proceeded to take a five pound smallmouth bass from the spot.

How did he know this was the spot I'd marked months earlier? Cross-triangulation.

Let's take a look at how it works. Cross-triangulation has been around as long as man. Using land references to get from Spot A to Spot B has always been how we humans make our way around. The same holds true when marking a good fishing spot.

Let's say the two stumps you found on the flat are something you want to be certain you remember. You know the depth they are in by doing some simple math: the lake is down 8´, when the water comes back to full-pool, the stumps will be in 8´ of water.

Once your depth has been established, you'll want to look for land references in every direction. You'll need above-water focal points that are easily seen.

Let's say that to the east there is a large tree on the bank. West, there is a fire tower. Those are two points of reference. North, we have a building, and south, we have a boat ramp. If you draw two mental lines from your focal points, they should intersect and "mark" your spot.

You will now need to know the depth of the water your boat should be sitting in so you can make the best cast at the House.

Note: *I would mark this depth in three spots if possible to allow for wind direction and boat control.*

Chuck Moore and Richard Craig take time to study their maps before hitting the water.

The same process can be accomplished on natural lakes that do not have a draw-down period but a graph or flasher will be needed to accomplish these tasks.

Records are the most important pieces of fishing info that you can possess. Add some good hard and true trial and error, and your smallmouth bass fishing again increases 100%. (We're still aiming for that fifty-fifty odds ratio!)

Below is a simple system for recording your data. Add more to it when you find those little "extras" you find while out there fishing.

Date: _____

Times fished what time of day: _____

Place: _____

Time of year: _____

Baits: _____

Color: _____

Size: _____

Depth: _____

Water clarity: _____

Lake Level: _____

Barometric pressure: ❏ high   ❏ low

Cloudy or clear: _____

Structure/Cover: _____

❏ Baitfish on surface   ❏ no baitfish on surface

Number of fish caught/size: _____

Presentation of baits: ❏ fast   ❏ slow

Best bait of the day: _____

Wind speed (if any) and direction: _____

Game moving (rabbits, etc): _____

At times, we have those heavy rains that bring the water up. In these special cases, it's hard for a fisherman to resist moving up closer to shore along with the rising water. In some cases, the fish will move up with the water, but the smallmouth is a more *stay-at-home* kind of guy. He will move up after a few days, but those first one or two days after the rise … he will stay put.

This is where your cross-triangulation really comes in handy. If the House *was* in 8′ of water, and the lake came up 5′ … now the House is in 13′ of water. While everyone else is trying to find fish in that classic 8′ of water, you have your bait still knocking on the door in the right location.

Document that water rise in your efforts. Sometimes the door is open down a little deeper!

> **Note:** *Most lakes have governing web sites that include flow information and lake level listings. These should be part of your documentation processes. The information is ripe for the picking.*

Young Dusty Matlock and his dad, Larry, use cameras and maps to document their underwater finds. Don't you just want to fish that place?! ☺ Firm red mud, deep water access, and a gorgeous stump. Sounds like House to me!

CHAPTER THIRTEEN

Position and Presentation

In previous chapters, we've talked about proper *presentation* of certain baits. Most of those references dealt with perfect weather conditions where we were learning the craft of finding our four components of House. Now that we've got a few perfect casts under our belts, let's talk about *position* and *presentation* under more adverse conditions.

Since wind and current are only obstacles and not our enemies, calculating where and how to fish under these conditions will greatly increase our odds of catching fish. Presenting that bait on any given day is an important lesson. Add position to the mix and you'll double your odds of zeroing in on that big fish in his House. Am I going to talk about where to put the boat some more? Yep … and yet another piece of the big smallmouth puzzle will fall into place for you.

Let's assume that you've gone through your trial and error casts and you've found the Houses where the fish live. You've made those prior casts with Zara Spooks and timed those other jig/grub casts to perfection. Plus you've documented it all in your

Smallmouth journal. The next time you return to that same spot, you'll know where your first cast needs to be.

The three stumps on the side of a point, the fence row that runs off of the bank into deeper water, or the rock pile or weed bed where you formed your pattern will be the tried, tested, and true places of House. We know where these places are because we wrote them all down—we kept accurate records. We know what types of baits we want to throw and how we want to retrieve. The only thing we don't know is where we put the boat.

Let's look for just a minute at some of the mistakes the average fisherman makes when approaching these spots. I've made these mistakes, too, so you're not alone. Learning from mistakes is what separates the average fishermen from the tournament-winning specialists we hope to become.

One of the biggest mistakes is also quite common. I've seen this played out many times. A fisherman pulls up to a good spot after settling the boat down from full throttle. He'll make a cast and then try to get the boat in the right position. This angler now has his boat out of position, a big bag in his line, his bait not in the House, he's monkeying with the trolling motor and turning on his graph—and his first and most important cast is wasted ... *wasted*.

There is absolutely no benefit to this mistake. After all, we've kept records of this spot, we know the depth where we need to stop, and we know precisely where the first cast needs to be. So slow down and get ready *before* you cast. Stop farther away and make a long cast to get the kinks out of the line (and your body) before honing in on the House.

Position the boat and make those early casts properly. Place that bait in the House with full control so that you're ready when that subtle strike happens. Done correctly, that fish won't be in the House ... it'll be in your hands.

The questions you should ask yourself before you reach the spot are the questions that will make your day. These are the im-

Donald Paul pulls a colorful friend from his humble abode.

portant tidbits between *maybe* catching a fish and perhaps catching several in this one House.

Ask yourself the following:

- **Is today's barometric pressure low or high?**

    If it is low pressure, you'd better stop further away from the House—the area of influence has increased in size these days.

    If it's low pressure, should I make one or two casts with a top-water bait long before I get nestled to the perfect sweet spot? The answer is yes, yes, yes! Tease that fish off the couch of the House.

- **Which way is the wind blowing?**

    Depending on wind direction, you may want to line yourself up on the spot from a slightly different direction than you might usually fish it. The conditions are different. So too should be our tactics.

    If we properly documented our last trip, then we'll know our angle of attack for this one. Since we have *access to deep water* nearby, we should be able to effectively approach the House from many sides — depending on wind direction. If we absolutely must, we can slip in from the shallow side—down wind—and sneak in from the back.

    If the front door is locked, then knock, knock, knock on the back door.

Zeroing in on that last statement

When fighting the wind (not an enemy ... but an obstacle), try to keep the House between you and the wind. Anyone who's ever operated a trolling motor knows that facing into the wind is the only way to keep the rear end of the boat from passing you. Let it slide on by and nose yourself into the wind and pretend you're keeping your nose upstream in current. It's the same thing.

Put the nose of the boat where you want it, and the back will soon follow. It's that simple. Slide the front of the boat upwind (like up-current) and let the back go where it pleases. Fish however you can from there—front of the boat, back of the boat—side—whatever. Hold that nose held-fast in place and adapt.

If we look at the diagrams on this and the following page, we'll see that we sneak in from behind the wind (nose into it), keeping the House between us and Mother Nature's fury. In case you weren't keeping up … those three stumps in this photo are "The House." ☺

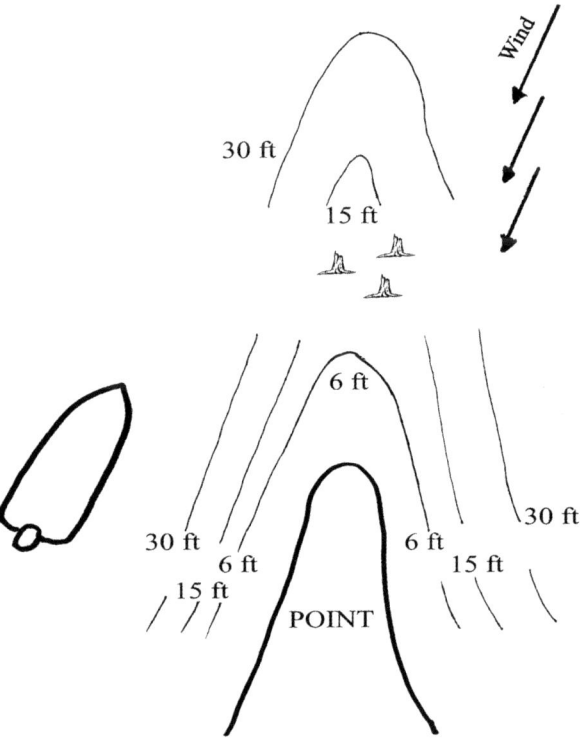

Now with wind direction in mind, two factors come into play; Where can I place my boat for the best control? And where can I place my boat for the best cast to hit the right spot and still be in control of my bait?

Long before you cut the engine and topple that trolling motor into the lake, you need to think long and hard about these questions. You need to see the big picture before you arrive. You know you have a good House, and more than likely a beautiful smallmouth bass has taken up residence in that spot—because it

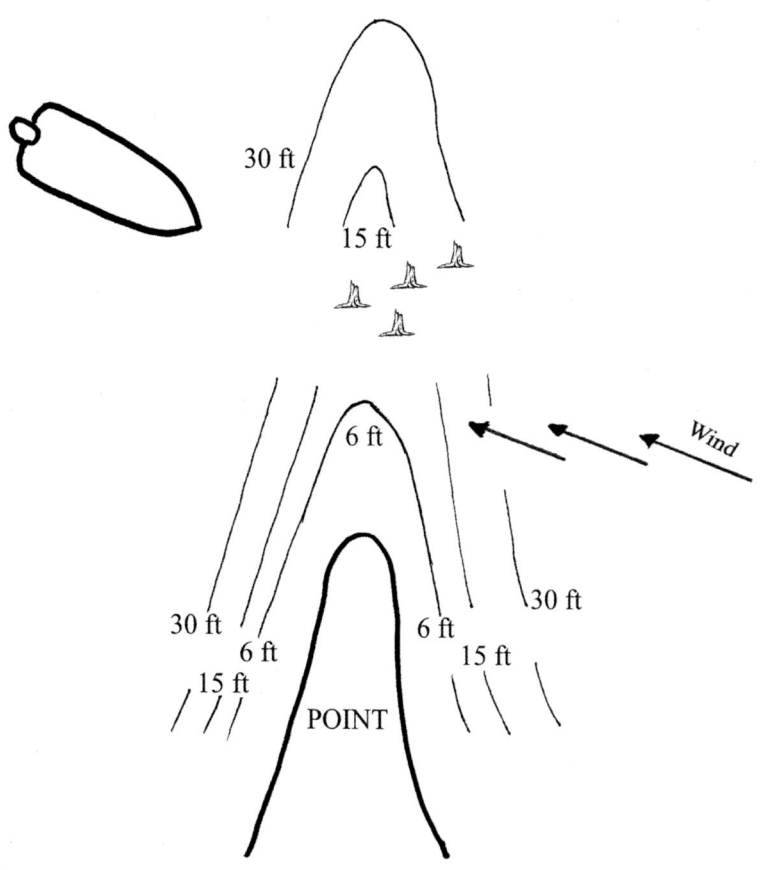

was the best House and she is big enough to move right in and muscle her way around.

Let's look at a similar view of the same point with a different wind angle.

While most of the places we mark as "big fish holes" are accessible from all sides, some are not. You will have to decide whether you can fish the spots under the conditions of the moment. Earlier we talked about going back into a cove first and fishing our way out … just because we could control our boat better. That's control. It's also part of *presentation*.

Now, lets look at the point where we were forming our patterns—the one where we found the three or four stumps on the point and we caught fish from them. We now know where they are, and we know what bait we want to use there. But what if we get there and the wind is blowing in such a fashion that we cannot position ourselves to make the best presentation?

I'm afraid that what we usually do is stop and make our casts anyway. After a few bad attempts, we turn to our fishing partner and say, "We can't fish this spot—let's go somewhere else."

Wasted time and wasted casts that's all I can say. You know it's a good House, but if you can't fish it properly, then move on. The lake is full of other houses in your record book. Slapping feverishly at a good House just because it's there doesn't make sense.

Fish it … or come back later and do it right. Don't waste your time with chaotic approaches. The weather will change—perhaps even on this day—and you can strategically address your special House without spooking the fish.

There were times over the years when I would slide in behind a windy point out of the wind and try to fish it from the improper angle. With the wind beating too roughly to use my top-water bait for test purposes, my choices dwindled down to the grubs, jigs, or bottom baits I could manage to throw.

This approach, though valiant and forceful, is a lot like the old adage "trying to push a chain uphill." When fishing from the shallow side into the wind, hang-ups and back-lashes come to mind—all in an effort to fish "against the grain". You might possibly accomplish this with a heavy spinner bait, bulky crank bait, or a giant spoon—but just remember you can always come back here and do it right later. Maybe you can find a way to get way upwind from the House and use the wind to help you reach the House from far away. It's not easy, but it's doable.

The main gist of what I'm trying to say is *use the wind … don't fight it.*

This big smallmouth is not about to give up its fight!

... All your work will be worthwhile ... You'll make a presentation that works and you'll know you've found House.

Welcome home!

Listen up, ya'll. This is a DEADLY chapter!

CHAPTER FOURTEEN

The Top Water Grub

Whoever heard of a top-water grub? Grub? Top water? It doesn't make usual sense. Nobody ever fished a grub on top of the water. That's nonsense. That's a figment of some crazy guy's imagination.

I suppose it is. I'm the crazy guy. And you know what? A top-water grub is DEADLY!!!!

Sit back and get ready for a fresh smallmouth lesson. I've kept this little personal tidbit of information safe and secret in my corner for years. It's helped me win tournaments—it's helped me make special days out of common ones. It's absolutely been a grand invention for me … just because I opened my mind and allowed my thoughts to roam free, making mountains out of mole hills.

Let me tell you about my giant mole hill. You're gonna love this one!

In all my years of fishing, I've relied on the grub for almost every situation. From the grub and lead-head, to a grub on the back of a spinner bait, I haven't found any situation yet where the grub has not produced. This is just one more super way to use our friend, the grub, in a deadly smallmouth situation.

When we talked about the best spots for smallmouth bass—stumps, humps, roadbeds, fence rows, flats and points—these were all a part of our master smallmouth plan. When we talked about brush piles, we backed off just a little and talked about those places as being not so favorable for smallmouth. Why was that? Because they're more likely a home for Mr. Largemouth rather than a smallmouth abode. It's a bit of a contradiction, but it *is* still possible to yank a smallie out of a brush pile. It's just not my first stop, as a rule.

Rules are meant to be broken … especially when the rest of the rules aren't producing. Yeah, it's a contradiction, but tournaments and challenges aren't won on compiling *only* systematic regiments. Yes, we've done our homework. Yes, we've documented our previous days. And yes … we've studied the rules of the House. But let's play a little! This is fishing. This is fun.

Let's toss a few odd-ball candies to our golden friends. This little trick is so much fun. I hope you can master it yourself … 'cause ain't nobody else gonna show ya. Let me tell you how it's done.

We all know that brush piles *can* and *will* hold a large number of fish. When you look at a brush pile just barely sticking from the water, or the one you mark with your flasher or graph, you can almost read the little signs on them that say, *fish me with a worm or spinner bait*. Both are excellent choices for this situation.

When you look at weed beds or moss-covered spots, you see these signs … *top-water weedless or a big jig*. Again, correct, but there is another method and it's fun as well … and just as productive, if not infinitely better.

Most of the grubs we've talked about so far have been 3" to 4" baits. Let's move to the 5" grub category and ponder a few things.

Without doubt this larger sized grub can be fished in all of the ways we've already talked about—lead head swimming or on the bottom. Now, let's go weedless and weightless.

As you know, brush piles are not my favorite places to fish for smallmouth, but I never pass up an opportunity to pull a bass from one of these areas. Bass, crappie, and many other species of fish find a happy home in this habitat. This means it's simply a fun stop along the smallmouth trail—one that can produce excellent fish.

I started fishing a grub as a top-water bait many years ago, and I mean *many* years ago. It dawned on me that there was brush in certain places and treetops in some locations that needed my attention. My days on the Susquanna River helped me hone my floating grub methods. Some of the bass I caught from the treetops of that river were caught on the top-water grub. I didn't mention it earlier because I wanted to save it for this chapter. This is a chapter different from anything you'll read about smallmouth fishing!

We fished the river that day, and we caught the fish outside of the tree itself (Smallmouth bass). We knew that there were fish to be caught in the treetops. As my fishing partner started to tie on a worm, I asked him, "Would you like to try something different just to have some fun?"

Of course, *yes* was the answer, and so begins the tale. I pulled a pair of 5″ grubs—amber pepper in color—and two 4/0 worm hooks from my tackle box. He looked at me in surprise when I rigged the grubs with no weight and the big hook arranged so we could fish it weedless.

"How do we fish this?" he asked. "Like a worm?"

"Well no … not exactly." I decided to show him rather than tell him.

We located a fairly large treetop lying in about 10´ of water. Its canopy was about 20´ out into the water away from the shoreline.

I rigged up the two grubs on spinning tackle with eight-pound test line along with the 4/0 worm hook. (When you rig a grub this way, always make sure the tail is up to create more action in the top-water situation. Hold your rod tip straight up in the air. This keeps the grub swimming nose-high and allows you to drop the rod tip to the water when the strike occurs). Never set the hook on the swirl of the fish, allow her to turn and start back

Note the slight upward bend to the grub and the upward-facing tail. The hook acts as a rudder while weighting it properly for the drop into brush. This is the proper hook rigging within the grub—tail up with a slight body arch.

down and tighten the line before the hook is set. This method also applies when you're swimming the grub in open water or over grass beds.

The large-sized hook in this rig serves two purposes; it matches the size of the grub and it acts as a rudder to keep the grub fishing in a realistic way while it keeps it from twisting your line.

I made my first cast to the end of the tree closest to the bank and swam the grub on top of the water, paralleling down the trunk of the tree until limbs were encountered. I then crawled the bait over the limbs (with no effort, the hook being attached weedlessly).

At the last minute before leaving the tree top, I flipped the bail, let out slack allowing the grub to fall through the branches, bouncing along as it wished (Always watch the line in these situations. You will have very little feel at this point, so your visual of the line is a big part of the game).

Shortly thereafter, I pulled the grub through the branches and back to the boat. I then cast again and repeated the process … but this time was different. As the bait swam down the same log again, a swirl came under the bait. I dropped the rod tip to the water, and after the line tightened, I set the hook. A couple of jumps later, a nice three-pound smallmouth bass came to the boat.

Next, it was my partner's turn. He pulled his grub across the water just beside some brush. The strike came, and he set the hook hard. That grub came flying by the boat like a bullet! We quickly assessed that he had set the hook too quickly. As soon as we learned that slow hook-set, we began to catch fish. In fact, some of the fish we caught that day came from casts made directly into the treetops. We simply allowed the grub to settle into those tree limbs, falling as it wanted, bouncing through the brush.

As you can imagine, we lost some of the fish we hooked because our line got tangled in the trees. But you know what? It's better to have *hooked* and lost, than to never have *hooked* at all.

Let me hang that fish, and we'll talk about getting him out of those trees next. It's all part of this fun game I call *Floating a Grub*.

This technique really comes into play in the brush and treetops you can't see under the water. In these cases, you start with the top-water swimming grub. When it reaches the treetop or brush pile, just allow the bait to fall into it. A grub with no weight and a big hook looks awfully good falling slowly through the water. With rod tip high in the air, allow the bait to fall on a slack line until the strike is detected. Then drop that rod tip quickly ... and when the slack goes out, set the hook.

This is not a technique you would fish all day long. It's just another form of fishing that will put an extra fish in the boat when it's needed—or entice that big fish from its brushy lair. Sneaky, huh?

Another place where this technique can be used is when bass are feeding in very shallow water, and you're already doing good with a grub and lead head. During these situations, we often find ourselves pulling our baits too quickly. In that shallow water, we're forced to pull that grub faster than we really want, just to keep if from snagging bottom. We can't keep the bait in the strike zone long enough to accurately present our bait to the fish.

I'm talking about those rare situations when the bass are extremely shallow—one to 2´ of water. Usually when this happens, we get all excited and throw anything we have tied onto our pole at the time. What we should be doing is taking the time to reach into our tackle boxes and pull out one of the grubs we've already rigged with no weight to make it top-water-ready. Having it handy and ready to use for those rare and special times will help you catch that fish!

Believe it or not, you can fish a top-water grub in as little as 6″ of water. It might even be of benefit to you to have this top-water special already tied on a specific rod in the boat so it's handy. I also like to play with this rig at first light and even right at dusk. It allows the fisherman to slow down and almost force-feed a smallmouth with patience and a very slow retrieve. It's presentation times ten! It's a tease!

I would suggest no larger than ten-pound test and spinning equipment for this technique. A 6' medium action rod seems to work best. It allows just enough height for a good swim of the bait, and it's short enough that it doesn't cause problems when fishing around sticks and twigs that just *love* to snap rod-tips. We've all been there before!

My choice of rods is always one that's just as long as necessary and not a bit longer. I know that very long rods work wonders for fishing the trees and brush when you need perfect placement with a long reach of the arm and rod. But why would you use that rod when you can just make a cast and let that bait settle on its own? There is a time and a place for every fishing rig—bait, line, and rod. Use each to your advantage.

I've used those long rods back in the brush many times. But whenever possible, I choose to make a simple and fun cast with my weightless grub.

Floating a grub. Whodda thunk it?

I suppose we've covered all of our three points thoroughly enough, but I want to go back to number one, just one more time.

I firmly believe that a smallmouth bass is much more likely to be spooked at home (high pressure) than she is when on the prowl (low pressure). Therefore, pulling in too closely to a spot is a bad thing. In most cases, once I've learned how to fish a certain spot, my first cast might be 15´ from the front or back door of the House—and low or high pressure has no affect on this decision at all.

I know that goes against what I've just told you, but let me explain. My desire to fish just outside the usual realm is a gut-instinct. It's just a feeling I get from experience. The closest comparison that comes to mind is an old largemouth mistake made by many. It's the equivalent of finding a treetop on the water's edge and throwing a plastic worm in the middle of it. Bang! You catch a largemouth. While you caught this particular fish, you probably just spooked everything else in the area around the tree getting the fish out of that trashy mess of sticks and brush.

My approach is to "beat around the bush" a little first! Start around the edges a little further out, then when you hang a fish you may get him away from the tree top without spooking the others. Another cast—another fish.

The same thing applies to the smallmouth bass. You must assume there might be more than one fish in or around the House. (She could have friends over for lunch!) Pick them off one at a time! Again, this type of fishing can produce many varieties of fish from the same House.

Of course, the distance you stop from the House will be up to you. These are not things that can be typed into a book. They will come to you through experience. When those subtleties do come to you (and they will), all your work will be worthwhile. You'll jot down those notes in your journal and use that precision information in years to come. You'll make a presentation that works and you'll know you've found House. Welcome home!

Steve Bernstein of St. Louis, Mo., left, and I, had the kind of bass fishing day that most can only dream of. When you're on a big fish smallmouth bass hole, it's not unusual to take a big largemouth bass at the same time. They will never out number the big smallmouth bass fish on the same hole.

Patience is a virtue ...

The longer the bass is aware of the bait the higher your odds of catching the fish.

CHAPTER FIFTEEN

Baits on the Bottom

This chapter will use part of what we've already learned in our grub lessons. I've talked about fishing the grub in order to mimic both food sources on the same cast, and now we're going to take that just a little further.

Remember, we've learned that as long as the grub is swimming through the water, it's a minnow to the bass, but when the grub is being tugged along the bottom, it becomes a crawfish. When you're trying out patterns and do both at the same time, you're increasing your odds of forming a pattern sooner by finding out which food source they prefer today. You're basically creating a smorgasbord buffet of food sources with one cast.

You'll also need to remember that if the day is high pressure, the preferred bait will be something fished very close to the House, as slowly as possible to keep that bait near the fish for the longest amount of time. If it's a low pressure day, things can move much faster.

For the purposes of this chapter, whether we're fishing slow or fast, we're fishing on the bottom.

As you learned previously, you're going to make your cast and allow your grub to settle to the bottom. Pick the rod tip up and retrieve at the same time. During the retrieve, drop the rod tip to the water, and let the grub sink back to the bottom to becomes a crawfish. All of this is done with a continuous, slow, steady retrieve. We talked about this at length before, but what we didn't discuss is what to do if the pattern lends itself to *bottom presentation*.

The grub is a fine bait to work on the bottom. Grubs were and will always be meant to swim—they just look great with that characteristic wiggle action. If you keep it moving, even slowly, the grub does most of the work for you. When that grub has told you that the fish want something on the bottom—we have to have one of those rare flashes of brilliance (Three in the same book, that has to be a record for me).

You're probably wondering why we'd change from our usual grub retrieve and start fishing on the bottom in the first place. This situation is yet another piece of the overall fishing puzzle.

Example:

We've tried our pattern test with the top-water bait and the grub. We've found that one of the test casts is catching fish at a certain depth and on certain pieces of cover or structure. We know this because the grub was taken while on the bottom. In this short time we've discovered three pieces of the puzzle from one type of cast.

We now know:

1) We're going to make our presentation on the bottom.
2) There is a bottom conducive to the fish.
3) We're in the House.

My friends, Nolan Ryan and Danny Darwin, pitchers for the Astros, enjoying a day fishing.

Knowing these three things, we want to take advantage of these types of spots to the best of our ability. Keep the bait in front of the bass as long as possible and give it a natural look. Let's say the pattern we found with our tests is stumps in 10′. You'll want a bait that can work naturally in these spots for a long period of time. Remember, you're knocking on the door of the House.

In this situation, hard as it is for me to say, I'll take the grub off my line and start fishing a bait I can keep in the same spot for a longer time. An artificial crawfish or a 4″ worm will work well. These baits don't require the faster retrieve for action. I want something that can lay on the bottom of the House without looking conspicuous.

I might also tie on a hair fly with a number 11 pork frog on the back. I want something made for smallmouth bass that can be fished slow. These baits can be hard to deal with if your patience level is off. Sometimes you need to leave a bait in the House long enough to go and have breakfast, then when you return, just set the hook. Live bait fisherman have done this for years because they knew the exact spot to place their bait.

Another story comes to mind …

My friend, Conrad, and I were on Percy Priest Lake one night fishing for smallmouth bass on one of our favorite holes. There was no wind, so we could keep our boat in position for a long time with little or no effort. Conrad, for some reason, had put a ¼ oz. hair fly tipped with an Uncle Josh number 11 pork frog on a casting reel with twelve pound test line.

After a few casts, the long-expected bird's nest infected his reel. Conrad sat for what seemed like an hour before he finally freed the nest and began to reel in line. As he reeled in, we noticed that the line seemed to be further on the other side of the boat than before. In fact, you could see the line shinning in the black-light rays. As the line started tightening up, he quickly decided that the bait was *not* hung on the bottom. He set the hook, and began his fight.

In the eerie blue shade made by the black-light, six pounds of smallmouth began its quest for freedom—jumping, lunging, and thrashing in an attempt to get free. After a good fight, Conrad lipped the fish. We looked her over good and released her.

Conrad's comments made sense. "I wonder just how long it took before the fish took the bait? I know the bait was in the right spot even with the backlash."

With that question in mind, we began to test the water by placing bait where we wanted it and just letting it sit. I can tell you right now this was like sitting in your backyard and watching grass grow, but we gained some important knowledge.

What we learned was that if we let the bait sit in the same spot for one or two minutes and then barely moved the rod so as to make the bait barely move, we would get the strike. When we worked the bait faster, we still caught fish but it took more casts. It was like the fish just swam over, eyeballed the bait, and when it twitched, she struck—like the fish was just daring that little crawfish to move.

During that night we tried this technique many times, and it worked a high percentage of the time. Later, as the wind came up, it didn't work as well because we couldn't control the situation like we could with no wind.

It all goes back to the weather conditions that night. It was a high pressure night, so the area of influence for the bass had decreased. The longer the bait remained in the House—the better our chances were for a hook-up. You know … I guess you could compare this to some of those nature shows where the lion makes a kill, feeds for a while, and then lies down close to her dinner. She's content with that until some animal comes by and tries to take a bite.

Do smallmouth bass allow the bait to just be there like the lion, and when another fish gets close decide to hit? Or is she just looking the bait over, waiting for it to make that one twitch that sends her over the edge? I really don't know, but I do know it works.

If you want to satisfy your curiosity about this, the next time you go to an outdoor show watch the presenters throw their baits into the tank. In most cases, they won't start to move their baits the moment they touch the bottom. They wait, then when the move takes place, the strike occurs. In other words, the longer the bass is aware of the bait the higher your odds of catching the fish.

Uncle Grady taught me to have patience, and my buddy, Conrad, helped me figure out a way to utilize it.

*In fishing, as in life,
dance when it matters,
and bounce in the House
when there is competition nearby.*

CHAPTER SIXTEEN

Bouncing the Jig

While I like the drag-and-feel approach to fishing a hair jig, there are times when the bouncing method will produce. I don't use it often, but I do practice this system on a few very specific situations.

As we know, the favorite food of the smallmouth bass is crawfish—but the primary food *by volume* is the minnow. Knowing this allows us to evaluate a potential fishing spot with better efficiency. When we pull up on a site we want to fish, and there are numerous baitfish swimming nearby (either visually or on sonar), we can assume that we'll have to be aggressive to entice a smallmouth to bite *our* bait over the countless other meals swimming down there.

We have to find a way to make our bait look better than the thousands of live fish swimming nearby. This condition (a difficult one) is where I employ the *bouncing-the-jig* technique.

When baitfish are plentiful, you really only have two choices … use a bait that imitates a minnow—like a crank bait or grub—or go to the bottom with the jig and catch the big one that's lying in wait.

For the most part, smallmouth have a 180° vision range, but they also have a narrow range of binocular vision that gives them depth perception.

With this heavy minnow activity present near the House, it's hard to catch fish on the hair jig ... *unless* you employ the bouncing technique. Our main goal is to make the fish aware that there is another food source readily available and more to their taste. More importantly, though, we're making that jig more visible to them by bouncing it. *Look at me! I'm the minnow you want!*

I guess you could say it would be like a hunter sitting by a tree during deer season. Hunters look in the direction they think the deer will be traveling. Humans have a limited amount of vision to the side—nearly a blind spot—until we catch a movement and our brain takes over and says to turn and look. Once we're aware of the movement, our attention is aimed in a different direction. This is what happens with the smallmouth bass when we distract them from those other food sources.

I have a slightly different method than most use, especially those fishermen that have a certain way of bouncing bait for Largemouth. Sometimes, Largemouth fishermen dance their baits over large areas simply trying to entice that fish from a large territory. Largemouth tend to be shallower, for the most part, and can see a bait from quite a distance. Smallmouth tend to hold-up closer to their House cover.

For the most part, I'm fishing for smallmouth bass in a very precise spot pinpointed by my past good record keeping. In most of these cases, the spot (House) is not that large, so too many bounces and my bait will be too far from the House. This is very unlike the bait-on-the-bottom technique where the offering is left resting there for a longer time.

When you see fishermen on TV bouncing a jig, it's usually one bounce before they allow the bait to settle back down—and after a short time, they bounce it again.

MY GOOD FRIEND AND FISHING PARTNER

Grand Ol' Opry Super Star, Porter Wagoner. I still miss him every time I hit the water. On a plane flight to one of our Arizona fishing trips, together we wrote "White Top Hell", an eerie little bluegrass song he recorded shortly thereafter. Those fish, that trip, and that song made wonderful memories.

When I'm bouncing a jig, I make three bounces all in unison, with no pause until after the third bounce. After all, I pretty much know where the fish should be, and I am trying to get its attention. It's just like the deer—it moves and you know something is there. You turn because you were not looking in that way to start with. It moves again, and you are able to zero in on the spot … and the deer. If you see the horns on the deer, then great! But one more movement will tell you for sure.

I believe it's the same way with bass. The three bounces are going to do one of two things—entice the fish to strike, because she is fully aware of the presence of the bait—or scare it to death, because something on the bottom is jumping up and down in an unnatural manner. So, using this method there's a 50/50 chance you'll spook the fish. I only use this when I feel like I have to. It's not natural. It's not normal. It's only *alluring*. I use it when other tricks are not producing.

Since I know where the House is through documentation and practice, I'll determine where I need to hop the jig three times before I am out of the strike zone.

Example:

Let's say there are ten stumps in a 25' radius—hopping the jig four times (four sets of three bounces) will usually cover the area.

On the other hand, if I have an isolated stump on the end of a point, one three-series hop may be all that's needed. We're trying to get the fish's attention, and the smallmouth bass is very aware of its surroundings.

After I hop the jig three times, I'll usually let the jig lie in the same spot for at least thirty seconds before repeating the process, that or I move the jig completely out of the area.

How high are the hops? I usually hop the lure with short and subtle tugs. The longer the hop, the faster it moves from the strike zone. It's your call, but try to keep it in the House as long as possible.

Hopping that jig or grub is a technique … not a way of swimming the bait through the House. It's a simple little dance to entice the fish. Then, let it lie before tugging it out of the House. There is simply no sense in dancing without an audience. Wait a little … and bounce again before leaving. Then start over with your new cast. Make every cast count in the House. Bouncing that bait all the way back to the boat will only make your arm tired from bouncing … not from catching fish.

This approach is a definite line-watching situation. Most of the strikes will occur on the fall, so after you determine what the bait *feels* like, when it *feels* different, set the hook. Setting the hook is free. I'd rather make an unnecessary hook-set than miss one! It's win-or-lose. I can always make another cast into the House. Since we lose a little *feel* with this method, we need to take extra precaution and set that hook when in doubt.

I'd like to add one more thing about this hopping technique that you might find amusing, but it's also very serious. I'd rather hop a bait into a House than throw the bait there and wiggle it. I believe that bass are wary and easily spooked, so dancing *into* the House is far better than an abrupt and startling jump into it.

We know that the longer a fish has to look at something, the more likely it will decide *not* to bite. With this approach, though, we're doing two things: presenting food in an obvious and intentional way, and invading that fish's territory and intentionally making a scene. Both cases are a win/win situation for the fisherman.

In fishing, as in life, dance when it matters, and bounce in the House when there is competition nearby.

Jim Ewell, long-time trainer for the Houston Astros, proving baseball and Bass do go together!

CHAPTER SEVENTEEN

Nighttime Smallmouth Bass

Fishing for smallmouth during the nighttime hours is really only an obstacle for the fisherman, not the fish. Bass react almost the same way in darkness as they do in the daytime. There are only a few subtle differences.

Basically, when it's dark, smallmouth are on the prowl for food. They seize this opportunity to eat during the eerie solitude of post-light. When fishing at night you'll need to remember that the *time* of night is important, timing and the area of influence each come into play, and where and how you fish the House is also a big consideration.

Starting with the simplest observations, fishing the House at night is much like fishing it during a perfect low-pressure front. Conditions are remarkably similar to those special low pressure, wide-feeding zones when the bass is roaming and comfortable in his surroundings. It's time to feed for the old rascal and he'll venture much further away from the House than on those blue bird days of sunshine and high pressure. Even though it might be a high pressure day, he should still feel considerably more comfortable in the darker hours after sunset.

If fish are sticking close to home (perhaps a 10' circle around the House), nightfall will likely find that fish more than three times that distance from his home. The cover of darkness has shaken some of his high-pressure woes. In fact, there may be times when numerous fish and their areas now overlap, making the fishing area even more productive.

If two, three, or even four areas of influence overlap, our dark hours of fishing will produce far more fish per spot. We might fish all night, toying with difference areas of influence of a handful of fish on one spot. With Old Man Sun out of the picture, we can zoom in on our areas of influence with much less hard work per cast.

With this in mind, my first casts of the night will be far beyond the perimeter of the House and not directly into it. It's similar to fishing that tree top—never throw into the tree first … go around the edges, picking off the outside fish before disturbing the House.

Time of night:

For many years, I've fished at night when the heat of summer drives me into the air-conditioning. These quiet and darkened hours of summer nights are the most peaceful time to fish. A certain calm engulfs the lake, foreshadowing an eventful fishing night.

To be successful as a nighttime fisherman, think about the smallmouth like he's a human being. We come in from work, sit down and relax for a while, take a shower, have dinner, watch a little TV, or go back over some of our old bass records—then we turn in for the night. Easy enough.

Now let's look at Ol' Man Smallie. He works hard most of the day defending his area of influence and feeding when opportunity arises, then he goes back home to relax and isn't in feeding mode. Unlike humans, he doesn't pull the lever on the recliner and shift himself into neutral, pretty quickly his predatory instincts take over and he starts prowling again. He's now the nighttime pride lion.

I use the term pride lion for a reason. Nature programs on television show pride lions (and many other wild animals) in their natural habitats, and most hunt at night. It's a common thread shared with most wildlife. Prey usually slows down during the dark hours, and predators sense that subtle change.

The higher-ups on the food chain gear up when the sun goes down. Smallmouth, being higher up on the fish food chain, as well as being larger than most other predatory fish, have few enemies to fear in the darkness. They feel safe in their superiority and they're fearless.

This is a good thing for us anglers. We can, as fisherman predators, hone in on our smallmouth target, much like it targets its own prey. Knowing that nighttime is a rewarding time to fish, we must now focus on how to fish each House … and at what time.

A lot of my success through the years has come from my studies of time and place in the House of the smallmouth. I've made countless notes and logged them all into my journal. Then I reviewed these tidbits of information and pieced them together like a puzzle. When I was done, I noticed a few correlations that seem to favor certain times of night and certain types of House.

Here is the knowledge gleaned from my notes:

- **Stone Houses.** Smallmouth tend to leave rocky cover earlier in the evening. I hit these holes early, aiming for that first nightfall prowl from the House.

- **Wooded cover.** Smallmouth tend to stick closer to House when home is a wooden abode (stumps, trees, etc). Though good all night long, these places are ones I save for when I've exhausted my early night spots like the rocky shoals.

- **Shallow pockets.** My next move is to the back of pockets … those coves with fresh water running in—enticing baitfish to gather. Bass travel from their normal House to these backwater covers in search of those baitfish enjoying the new current flowing into the body of water.

- **Long points beyond the backwater shallows.** As the moon rises, I'll slide on out to those pretty points, hoping to find where the baitfish have lured our smallmouth predator. Once they leave those shallower backwaters, long points closer to deeper water will be the next move for Mr. Smallmouth.

- **Back to House.** When the morning sun begins its rise, I'll find my way back to House. The bass will have made their prowl. They'll have strayed as far as they're going to. Like the Vampires in the movies, our little golden friends will be finding their way back to their coffin boxes we call House before Old Man Sun smiles on them. Rap on the door with my favorite top-water Zara Spook (Spook … get it?). Those scaly vampires are ripe for pickin' at the break of day.

Determining the perfect time of night to fish each spot is the hardest part of ironing out the nighttime puzzle. Your usual hot spots may not produce at certain times at night. Those fish might not be at home precisely when you arrive. They might be out prowling! Dig deep into your records and find the pattern and movement during certain hours of night.

Try the spots I've just mentioned in the order I've given them and record your results. Good or bad, you can never have too much information for your records. You'll be surprised to find that bad news recorded in your journal is just as important as the good. Knowing what didn't work can be just as important as knowing what did.

Write it *all* down. Write too much. You might be amazed by a connection to something as simple as the time of night or how brightly the moon was shining. Learn the system and try each place at different times of night. Just because a spot didn't produce at 10:15 doesn't mean it won't at 2:30. Stick around long enough to find out. Many fishermen tend to "run and gun," and never truly allow enough time to accurately fish a good spot. Don't move on *just* before the right time or right cast is made.

Another little story ... I just love little stories

Back in 1989, my friend, Conrad, and I were on Percy Priest Lake just outside of Nashville. It was one of those good nights with just a little breeze and calm water. We'd brought a cooler filled with food and a thermos of coffee and were ready to fish. We'd been fishing some of our good holes, and had stopped at one in particular that usually produced in the daytime.

It was early when we stopped on the small stump field just off of a long stretch of a rocky mud bank that led into about 10' of water. It was one of those holes had always seemed to be the ticket during the daytime, but the nighttime bass on this spot somehow managed to elude us.

We fished this spot with no success. So, about 8:30 we both had decided it was time to move on to our other holes that seemed to produce better in darkness.

As the night progressed into early morning and our fishing passion was starting to wane (as was the coffee), we headed back in. As we passed that same old stump field, I suggested to Conrad that we try it one more time.

When we stopped, Conrad picked up his spinning rod and reel with a 3/16 ounce hair fly tipped with an Uncle Josh no. 101 pork. One minute into his cast I heard him fighting a nice fish. Five pounds of smallmouth was tugged to the boat. Our blacklight glowed eerily as he released that beautiful fish.

It wasn't long before we had boated and released six fish—the smallest weighed in at four pounds. We had stopped there the second time at 2:30 in the morning.

We came back to that spot at that same time on many other nights. It was a big fish hole. Over the years, we caught many smallmouth bass from this spot and hardly any of them weighed less than three pounds.

As I've said many times, "There are big fish holes and little fish holes." This hole was the big one. Conrad and I named this spot *"The 2:30 Stumps."* Its name and time were both perfect.

Over the years, Conrad and I developed many spots like that where *time* was as important as the bait we were using. A good spot is a good spot. Change your timeline when things don't seem to work for you. Change your clock and you just might change your creel.

Baits at night

Some things never change in my smallmouth bass timeline/lifespan. But the bait colors do change … and I'll tell you why.

Some of my favorite color choices for nighttime are rarely used during daylight hours. At night, the darker the bait color—the better it is in most cases. I hardly ever use the chartreuse or green baits at night. I rely heavily on the browns and blacks, with brown being my favorite.

I'm sure it comes as no surprise that I love to use flies at night. For years, I have relied on the fly to catch smallmouth bass in the nighttime hours. If I broke down the percentage of bass caught on all the baits I use at night, the fly and pork frog would probably account for about 80 percent.

I've put together several color combinations that work for me in different sizes, from 3/16 ounce on up to 1/4 ounce. I try to keep a small array of those colors in my tackle box, much like I do for daytime fishing. This way I can create many combos with only a few different flies, sizes, and colors.

Again, I like those dark colors—black, brown, and even purple. I sometimes vary the shades of each, depending on the amount of light from the moon. It might be just my preference, but I mix and match the purple flies with the brown pork, and vice-versa. I might even tie on a black fly with a brown grub.

Whichever you choose, I suggest keeping these different combos in the tackle box, just like the daytime color combos. Being able to make countless color combos with just a few colors of each grub, fly, and weights is a nice option. Keep those few special colors handy. You can remove a purple pork frog and thread-on a brown grub quickly. It just might make the difference.

Nighttime top-water

On those nights when the lake is calm and the moon is bright—when the water looks like glass—it's time to bring those ornery prowling fish to the surface. Top-water is not a technique you use with every cast on these nights, but in certain situations it will produce seriously big fish—those aggressive monsters we're looking for. Just as we did with our test pattern casts on a new point in daylight, we'll do the same in darkness, with a few variations.

When I reach my destination spot, I probably won't pull out that Zara Spook rod that I keep handy at all times. This top-water presentation I'm about to give will reflect two things.

- **Number One** — I'll probably throw a noisy, splashing buzz bait to churn up the water and catch Mr. Bass' attention. I might use a chugger type of bait, too. We want something to catch the glimmer of the moon on the lake surface, making waves as it goes, thrashing the water surface. The noise is a wake up call for the fish. I like this method a lot, but on some nights, the buzz bait is just too noisy—almost startling to the fish. On these nights, I zero in with number two.

- **Number Two** — The top-water grub. On high pressure nights when the fish are easily startled, that little ripple on the surface created by my floating grub is *just right*. It will entice the fish on the bottom that's staring up into the moonlit night. That floating grub is just plain deadly, day or night.

I keep a floating grub tied on one pole, and usually a chugger type bait tied on another. With both handy, I can be ready at a moment's notice. Sometimes I use both baits on the same spot. It's not uncommon for me to settle into a good spot and toss that top-water grub first. It's not as noisy, and in my opinion will have a better action. If three or four of these casts fail to produce, I'll make one long cast with a chugger to wake those fish up. If no fish take the bait then, I'll switch to my fly and go to work using my fly-and-rind techniques.

It's hard to beat the hair fly or tube bait at night. *You know I love that fly!* I usually make my retrieve on or near the bottom. At night, the working of the fly on the bottom fills 95 percent of my time. I just like it there. It seems to produce better for me. Either those fish are racing toward that top-water bait, or hugging close

MY SON, JAY, AND FISHING LEGEND BILL DANCE

Bill's kind words and great knowledge have been a wonderful credit to the fishing industry. Thanks, Bill. You'll always be a class-act in my book.

to the bottom. Though smallmouth bass are opportunists when feeding on minnows, they certainly set their sights on crawfish that are searching for *their* food at night. Therefore, the bottom working fly has by far the most appeal.

Your presentation may still be the same slow, in-House, on the bottom movement, or it may not. Just as in day fishing, the fish will tell you how fast the bait needs to be fished.

When day fishing, I almost always start out fishing slow, and work my way faster given the need. When fishing at night, though, I tend to fish a little faster, knowing in my heart that these fish are prowling and more likely to be active and aggressive toward my bait presentation.

Of course, I'll adjust as the night moves on, either speeding up or slowing down my retrieve as I find the speed that suits the fish at each spot and at each time of night. I might even record some of my findings on my recorder, just so I don't forget. It'll make the next night's fishing that much easier, once I study what I've learned.

Some states do not allow fishing at night. You'll need to check your local regulations and ask around. The game officials can offer insight on proper ways to be both productive and safe. Safety is paramount. One little problem on the lake at night can be disastrous. With so few others on the lake to help, darkness is a lonely and dangerous place to be if problems occur. Practice proper boating laws and safety techniques and you'll live to fish another day. As enjoyable as night fishing is, it is also quite dangerous. Keep that in mind and your experience on the water will be wonderful.

I'm sure you've guessed that the ability to *feel* at night is a must. If daylight *feel* is important, you can imagine what a big deal it is when the light is gone. To help your night fishing presentation, check on the use of black lights that are made for night fishing. If you've never fished with these fun toys, I hope you soon get a chance.

Certain monofilament lines are illuminated like giant purple ropes with black lights. It's really quite amazing if you've never witnessed it. Every little twitch is noticeable. It gives the added visual aid to go with your ability to *feel*.

When fishing at nightfall, keep in mind that the only real difference between the daylight hours and dark is that the fish are usually more alert and aggressive. We fishermen merely need to navigate safely and utilize what we've learned to make our nighttime casts beneficial.

After all, ya'll …
fishing is supposed to be fun.

CHAPTER EIGHTEEN

The Four P's of Fishing

A lesson learned with Rock Bass and friendship

Most avid smallmouth bass fishermen don't consider the Rock Bass or Red-Eye a sporting game fish. Most lump those smaller smallmouth cousins in with the Bluegill and the Perch. It's just a fish for the skillet and nothing more.

For those anglers looking for a truly fun day, though, these little giants of the bass world can be a blast. One trip to the river with me in late spring would make believers out of most of you. Sure, most of these fish don't weigh more than a pound or so, but are bigger, and they put up one wickedly-fun fight. They're the little brother to Old Man Smallmouth, and I love to catch them.

Some days I'm a serious smallmouth man. Other days, I can wade the creek and relax in one of my favorite environments, catching Red-Eye and catchin' rays knee-deep in cool creek current. We start our spring Red-Eye fishing in late April and fish well into early summer, enjoying this fishing game when our smallmouth are locked up and bedding on the lakes.

It wasn't until I took my good friend, Carl Haley, out one day that I realized just how special our local winding creeks can be to those who've never been fishing there. Carl is a novice at fishing, but has been an outdoorsman all his life. When my son, Jay, and I took him to the river for some Red-Eye action, he had a great time. His words said it all, "I've got to do more of this!"

After all, ya'll ... fishing is supposed to be fun. We had fun that day.

The Creek Fishing Experience

At the risk of losing my smallmouth readers, let's talk about that taboo—rock bass of the creek—and use what we learned in our serious smallmouth fishing to catch some. Carl, Jay, and I will let you tag along ... (Somebody's got to carry the stringer!)

We started our morning with a quick lesson in catching live crawfish to use as bait. In some states, this is not a legal practice, but our Tennessee waters are still legal as crawfish seining areas. It's possible to catch a few crawfish by hand, turning over rocks and logs in the creek, but a far better method has been used for decades ... the seine.

Proper seining isn't a difficult thing with a few simple tools. All you really need is a small seine, a bucket, and well ... a creek.

We started our bait catching way up in the small creeks, those easy to wade and only a few inches deep, where both banks can easily be reached by the length of our seine. A seine takes two people to operate it—Carl and me on this day. We hold the ends of the seine downstream from the many little shoals of the creek, but still very much in the current.

Once this is in position, another person (Jay on this trip) walks in the creek upstream, turning over rocks and debris. As the muddy water from the upstream agitation flows downstream toward our

Jay Bean and Carl Haley on the river, sporting some dandy Rock Bass

open net, minnows, crawfish, and snails swirl downstream, too. In a matter of a few minutes, hundreds of crawfish pile up in our simple little seine. We toss out the minnows (a legality) and any accidental bluegill, snails and debris. The remaining crawfish are scooped up and placed in our waiting minnow buckets.

These same minnow buckets will soon be attached to our belts further downstream when we can allow the bucket to float in the fresh water. This allows us quick access. These little crawfish are the perfect bait for our day of wading the creeks and fishing.

We've fished many creeks in Tennessee in just this way. We loved the upper Harpeth River, the Buffalo, and others like the Piney. They are all good for those fun little Red-Eyes and the occasional smallmouth.

For over thirty-five years, my son, Jay, has caught Red Eye and smallmouth on this one little old spot in the river. That smile tells all ... the river is his second home.

We thread our crawfish onto a small jig head by hooking it through the tail from the bottom up. That way, as the crawfish crawls along, the hook stays away from most snags. Also, it helps hook the fish in the upper lip, right where you want it.

Prior to our morning on the water, Carl had been reading the infant stages of this book. He'd studied it before we left and did his best to utilize what he'd read by practicing in the creek. He

Jay and a fiery little Rock Bass That water is clear and beautiful behind him. Rivers are full of these playful Red-Eye Rock Bass. They're not difficult to catch and they're delicious in the skillet. Red Eye lessons learned on the river pay off at the lake.

was using what he'd learned about House and the importance of placing his bait in exactly the right spot, given current conditions and his new thoughts on *feel*.

Though a novice at fishing, Carl approaches everything in life wide-open. In seconds, he can find the best and fastest way to conquer his goal. On this day, his task was fishing for Red-Eye in the creek, and he learned a lot and loved his relaxing day on the water. Although he might not have realized it in the beginning, he was also learning tried and true smallmouth methods by simply wading the creek and observing. It was a great day for learning!

Carl's first few casts weren't quite perfect, but he got the hang of it quickly. Jay made one quick (and perfect) cast into the first hole we wanted to fish—and sure enough—bang! One cast, one good Red-Eye. Jay had targeted that one fish and managed to add it to his stringer before the fish spooked and darted away. It was lesson number one for Carl.

Presentation.

As we moved on to the next hole, Carl got the chance to observe several good Red-Eyes moving in and out of a structure. Seeing fish always makes a fisherman excited. His first cast missed slightly, but cast number two hit home dead-on, and Carl caught his first Red-Eye. (He had a death grip on the poor thing!) What fun!

A couple more holes downstream helped fill our creel and Carl was having a blast. Yeah, Jay and I were having just as much fun, but we'd been here before. Jay grew up with two wet feet, so this stretch of river was as familiar to him as his bedroom. Having Carl tag along as we visited our special place was just an added treat for us.

At the next hole, while Carl was still talking about his first Red-Eye, another form of creek cover came into play—a fallen treetop with slower moving water. Carl remembered from his reading that you never throw in the middle of the House on the first cast. He made the correct cast and another Red-Eye was in his hands. I believe his words were, "Man … this is great!"

Learning where the fish relate to structure was another lesson learned and proved.

Proximity

We soon spied another Red-Eye lurking beneath a rock ledge. Carl made his cast and hooked the fish just as he'd planned. Just as quickly as it took the bait, though, the fish got off his line. To our surprise, the fish went right back to the House. Using our polarized glasses, we could easily see the fish back at home in the House.

Another few perfect casts had the same fish back on the line. Then, to our surprise, another fish moved right in the House. Soon, Carl had picked that one from out of the House. Another lesson learned and two to go.

Patience and Persistence

For the last 25 years on the seminar circuit, I have always tied four things together. I call them *The 4 P's of Fishing*. Successful fisherman use these 4 P's to their advantage. They are:

Presentation
Proximity
Patience
Persistence

I asked Carl how he felt about his first creek trip, and his reply was, "It was just a lot of fun, and I feel like when I go back my fishing ability will increase from a three (on a ten-scale) to a big five. Now I know how to catch the crawfish and how to hook them properly. I now know where to look and how to line up on a certain spot, and I know that feel and watching the line is important.

"Those fish don't exist just everywhere in the creek—you have to find the right House. I also learned that when Jay moves out some distance ahead of you he is not doing that just to give you room … he's beating you to the good spots! He's fished these areas many times and he knows where he needs to go, just like your keeping records, it all ties together."

★★★

I wanted to add this segment into the book for two reasons. One, it was great watching Carl enjoying his first creek fishing experience. And two, I cannot express how important it is to learn everything you can to improve your fishing skills. The creek is just another one of the tools you can use to help yourself along the way.

Whether you're tossing a grub at smallmouth in a big lake or casting for Red-Eye in the river, the lessons learned and remembered will increase your odds of both catching fish and improving your fishing ability.

CHAPTER NINETEEN

Smallmouth Through the Ages

When we talk about the size and age of a smallmouth bass, we have to look at several different factors that determine the growth rate of the fish. They include the following:

• **Food Source**—The biggest factor in determining the size of a fish is the food source available to that fish in any given situation. When a smallmouth is young, its main food source is the population of zooplankton that live in nearly all rivers, lakes and streams. These are tiny crustaceans that are almost invisible to the naked eye.

As the bass grows larger, his attention turns more to the shad or minnow population. It's not until a little later in his lifecycle that the bass discovers the little fillet steaks crawling around on the bottom nearby … those tasty little crawfish.

While the crawfish is by far the favorite food source of the smallmouth bass, it's certainly not the most plentiful. Since the natural aim of the fish is to grow and stay healthy (and not get eaten in the process), the minnow or shad population becomes the number one food source due to its abundance. Lakes in Tennessee are blessed with a tremendous shad population that sustains a number of predator fish. Perhaps that's why so many species thrive and grow to such large proportional sizes in those waters.

- **Habitat**—Where the fish lives or habitat is another great influence on the growth rate of smallmouth bass. In most cases, reservoirs with little or no current will grow bigger fish than creeks or rivers. Flooding in these moving water areas forces fish to exert more energy to fight the current and chase a food source. As a smallmouth bass grows, his time spent in current decreases, therefore he exerts less energy and his growth may increase as a result.

There are exceptions to every rule, though, like Pickwick Lake in Alabama. This lake grows some of the best smallmouth bass in the world. When the dam is flowing, the current will tax any trolling motor. The bass in this high-current situation use the moving water to feed and flourish. When the current is down during a low generation schedule, a rest period begins.

Because the bass are not continually under the great stress periods from moving water like those in constantly-flowing creeks and rivers, they don't see a reduction in size. Quite simply, these fish get a moving water break now and then to rest.

- **Growing Season**—One other factor in the growth of a smallmouth bass is what I call the growing season. Fish are cold blooded, and when the temperatures plummet, the feeding cycle of the bass slows along with its metabolism. That's why a six year old smallmouth bass in Pickwick Lake can be more than 20″—while that same six year old bass in Ontario, Canada, may be only 13″ or 14″ in length.

Also, as a smallmouth bass gets older, the growing process slows somewhat. A smallmouth bass that's 10″ long and two years old may grow 6″ or more in the next two years. While a six year old, 20″ bass may only grow 2″ over the next two years. All of these factors also depend on the food source and the habitat.

It is a fishing fact that the majority of monster-sized smallmouth bass come from the south. Another little-known fact is that most northern smallmouth bass, even though they don't have the longest growing season, can—and I believe *will*—reach the same sizes given enough time.

For instance, northern bass have a longer lifespan than their southern cousins. Their *growing season* is shorter, but their *lifespan* is longer. I believe it's possible to catch a northern fish that's 15 years old, while 13 years is quite a stretch in the south.

The current world record smallmouth, caught by D. L. Hayes in 1955, was exactly as old as the lake in which it was caught. D. L.'s Dale Hollow smallmouth weighed in at a whopping 11 pounds 15 ounces and it was thirteen years old. Biologists pulled a scale from the fish and studied the growth rings to verify the age. Fish scales resemble "growth rings" in trees. That was one magnificent fish.

D. L. Hayes' and his 11 pound 15 ounce Dale Hollow Lake Smallmouth 1955.

I believe that Dale Hollow Reservoir will always grow bigger bass than most places just because of its geography. It has two great old-fashioned bass rivers feeding it, dumping clean water and good baitfish down into the lake waters. It's a natural wonder, created as much by God as by the Corps of Engineers.

On the opposite end of the spectrum, is Percy Priest Lake in Nashville, Tennessee. With all of its tremendous fishing pressure it will easily grow fish to the six pound size, but it is unlikely to produce a seven pound fish. Seven pounders have come from there, no doubt, but the likelihood is much less here than in other lakes with less intense fishing pressure right outside a major city.

What this all boils down to for fishermen is that we are dealing with a species that is better released than taken home to the skillet. I would much rather see my grandson have a chance to catch that bass three years later when she tips the scales a few pounds heavier. I suggest you take a photo and brag about the photo, not how tasty its fillet was hot out of the skillet.

I don't hold hard feelings for those who keep and eat smallmouth bass. Our game laws tell us that we have limits on what we can legally take, and I respect that. Knowledge of the fish and your ability to catch them will determine how many you will release back to the House and how many you will catch in the future.

Do you keep and mount a trophy? You bet you do. You've worked hard to attain the goal of catching that fish. But when you have that trophy on the wall, think about releasing the next one you catch. The feeling you get will always be with you, and it will be one you'll treasure … always.

Game and fish agencies make every effort to maintain our fisheries in a way so that future generations can have the pleasures of catching fish that we've enjoyed. The introduction of size limits and slot limits work in certain situations, but not all.

The spinner bait can turn some big smallmouth bass.

It concerns me that when a fisherman goes to a lake where the length limit is 18″, and he catches 15 smallmouth bass with only one or two over the limit, those two fish go home with him. The smallmouth bass photos that you see in this book—well, they all swam away when released back into the water.

When I was guiding, the limit per-person on smallmouth taken home as a trophy was *one fish*. Even with that stipulation, more than 90 percent of the fish caught were released back to the water.

Even when I fished smallmouth bass tournaments, I *never* fished one where the legal limit was so high that it was impossible to keep them healthy. Wherever I fished, I would recommend that the limit for the tournament be no more than three fish ... and 90 percent of those tournaments did just that. It made me happy. I won my share of tournaments, but I never considered myself a tournament fisherman.

I guess I may have wandered just a little far here, but my feelings about the smallmouth bass go much farther than I can type into the pages of any book. I have a passion for this fish and hope to instill that same love of species to those who enjoy the battle of hook and line like me. I hope that you get those same feelings when a five pound smallmouth bass is jumping with your son or daughter or even your grandchild is hooked to the other end. If they want to have the fish mounted the first time, it's what they deserve ... then the rest is up to both of you.

There is a fine line that determines when to keep that special fish and when to release it back into the wild. As sportsmen, it's our job to balance the scales and still enjoy our wonderful hobby of smallmouth bass fishing.

CHAPTER TWENTY

Spinner Baits, Crank Baits, and Worms

It's hard to have a conversation about bass fishing and not discuss the spinner bait. For years, I've chased smallmouth bass in just about every way—from the grub swimming through the water, to the top-water off of a long point in the early morning hours.

All of these are fun ways to catch smallmouth bass, yet there is another. Smallmouth, for the most part, are a deeper water fish. They seek out the deep holes for comfort temperature-wise, and they move to the shallows to feed if need be when light and temperatures dictate. While lots of smallmouth bass are caught in shallow water areas, the true smallmouth bass fisherman knows how to probe the depths for this mighty brown fish ... especially the bigger and heavier older fish we hope to catch.

Spinner baits are one way to accomplish this, both day and night. They work especially well at night when the fish are on the prowl in both shallow and deep water. Like most fishermen, I've got tackle boxes full of pretty lures. Those multicolored baits look good and spinner baits are no exception.

Even though I almost always use the same few lures I love, I still have that inner fisherman who wants *all* the colors and *all* the sizes of everything on the shelf! Yet, as my smallmouth bass fishing came of age, my choice of spinner baits changed as well.

When we first take a look at spinner baits, the smaller sizes look very appealing, like the eighth to quarter ounce models. Those work, but if you have trouble feeling, you'll feel the fish too late for a good hook set using this bait. I always say: *"If you can't feel the bait, you will never feel the fish when it hits."*

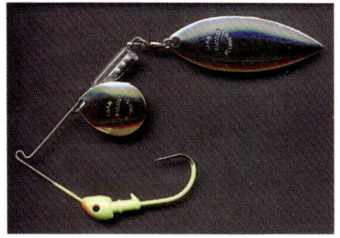

Stan Sloan's Aggravator spinner bait

When I tie on a Stan Sloan's Aggravator spinner bait, it is usually 1/2 to 5/8-ounce. These sizes allow me to fish this bait on the bottom where I want it to be—bumping into the houses where the bass live. It gives me the ability to feel the bait under any situation. *Feel* is the key, and if you think that a smallmouth bass won't try to take the rod from your hand (even with this large sized bait), you're wrong.

The size of the bait in this case is a new experience in fishing. If you've only used the smaller sizes before, you'll find these bigger sizes easier to fish *and* easier to feel.

The next time you go to your favorite fishing tackle store, pick up one—just to give it a try. Match it to a rod and reel that will handle the weight and hang on! Practice with the heavier bait and learn all you can about the feel and how it works. A new avenue of fishing will open up for you.

Crank baits, spinner baits and worms

By now, you know that I'm not all that fond of treetops and brush piles for the simple fact that the baits I rely on most seem to stay in the brush pile more than they come out—they get hung-up big time. I know these places produce fish on a large scale. You have also learned from this book that I am always looking for ways to make my time on the water productive. I love to float a grub over a brush pile and let it slowly fall into the branches. This produces strikes, but sometimes I just want to have a little fun. When I fish, sometimes I don't go to catch fish—but rather to see if they are there (in those spots) for later use. When I do this, I have these three baits tied on three different reels with some slight modifications: **crank bait, spinner bait, and worm.**

While these are not my number one baits for 90 percent of my fishing, they can be very productive for smallmouth bass—especially the spinner bait. So, let's take a look at a pattern I use just to have fun and catch fish.

The crank bait that I use must be a digger. While it is a fact that long narrow crank baits like Shad Raps, countdown, Rapalas are more suited for smallmouth. In this case, I want the big, fat crank bait that has a wide wobble and displaces some serious water.

The first thing I do is remove the treble hooks and replace them with one single weedless hook facing backward. This crank bait can be pulled through the limbs with hardly any hang-ups. You might have a harder time setting the hook in a fish, but that's not a necessity right now—because I am using this bait to see if these fish are in that House.

Example: Let's say that I get a strike on the crank bait …

The striking fish does not hook-up and never feels the hook. I lay the crank bait down, pick up the spinner bait and cast the outside edge of the tree or brush pile in random casts to see if I can bring the bass out. If this works, fine. If not, then I pick up the worm and make my cast directly inside the brush or treetop.

The worm color in this instance will be blue, blue on blue, blue with a blue tail, light blue, or dark blue.

You might be wondering, *why spend the time with the crank bait when I could just throw the worm or spinner baits?* Back in my tournament and guiding days when I had a trip or tournament the next day and I wanted to cover a lot of treetops or brush piles in a quick time, I would use the crank bait to find the fish, then let my clients have a shot at catching those fish the next day. I knew the fish were there, so the confidence level was high both for the client and me.

There is one more reason for using this method in the hotter months … when all else fails, it's just a plain fun confidence builder.

CHAPTER TWENTY-ONE

Approaching a New Body of Water

Over the years, I've had the privilege of fishing many bodies of water across the United States, and some in a few other countries, too. There is a lot of pressure to produce consistent strings of fish on these lakes that were new to me. But, without bragging, I made it work.

There isn't much difference between going to a new lake for the first time and going to your old lake after a month's layoff. Either way, you still have to find the fish again. The only real advantage you have on your familiar lake is some previous working knowledge of the lake and where you've been successful previously. You know some good places to start and you've established some habits for fishing this location.

Believe it or not, you might have a big advantage when fishing a new lake. You have no regular habits. You have no set-in-stone ideas already in your head. On this new lake, you're forced to go back to the drawing board and start fresh, and you'll have to employ two of the four P's—patience and persistence.

If you were to ask 50 different fishermen how they'd approach a new lake, you might get 50 different answers. But we can cut that down quite a bit because we're not just looking for fish—we're looking for smallmouth bass ... big ones.

In order to answer the question of how to approach a new lake, we have to consider a few of things.

1) How long do I have to fish, one day or three days?

2) What time of year is it?

That's a pretty short list, wouldn't you say? There are other factors involved, but the two listed above are the ones we have to consider the most. Time on the water is always a factor and different times of year call for different patterns.

Never let the amount of water overwhelm you

What happens when we get overwhelmed with the amount of water is we start fishing faster and faster ... which means we've probably lost our degree of control. The situation is controlling us, rather than we fishermen controlling our own destiny. I believe there are always alternatives to explore ... just do this exploring in a systematic way, utilizing your time on this new water in the most effective way. If you're in a rush to "wear out the water," you'll miss valuable opportunities to put fish in the boat.

Never go fishing for a limit—fish for a bite

Fish for fish—limits will come along later. After all, why does it matter? You're probably going to release the fish anyway. You have the knowledge to catch more.

Any good tournament fisherman will fish for bites way before he or she starts talking or thinking about a limit. You have to believe that you will find and can catch the fish in a new lake by having patience and using your smallmouth knowledge.

To accomplish this, you'll need to break down this new lake and see what makes it tick.

- **Time of Year.** The time of year will influence how you fish more than any other factor.
- **Type of Lake.** Across the country there are several different types of lakes that hold smallmouth bass. These include the canyon lakes of Arizona, grass-filled lakes of the north, and highland reservoirs of the south like Dale Hollow and Center Hill. Each lake is different, yet they all have one thing in common: They all hold smallmouth bass.

   The smallmouth bass in Minnesota is no different than the ones in Tennessee. They are smallmouth, simple as that, and they love something that is irregular in nature.

These are my ways of approaching a new lake—they're not the only ways, but these are ones that have worked for me for years. They'll work for you, too.

Fishing the fictional lake

Springtime Pattern

We have a late spring day on Lake Gotta CatchUm, located in the state of Patience. We have a three-day vacation planned here, and we want to spend day one finding our pattern. Once we find our patterns on this first day, we might zero in on better ways to consistently catch fish. But for this first test day, I will run-and-gun in a consistent and predetermined way.

Here are some of the things I would like to know before I get to the water.

1) What is the size of the lake?
2) Is this a man-made or natural lake?
3) How much fishing time do I have?
4) Is lake level falling or rising?

The size of the lake is a must-know so you can eliminate water. You can illuminate 95 percent of a lake just by looking at a good contour map.

If this lake is man-made, I'll concentrate on the areas closest to the dam. The water is usually cooler and deeper at the lower end of a man-made lake. If there are very distinct points on this end of the lake, I'll mark them on the map—especially if they drop off quickly into deeper water.

The point could be 50 yards long and 15´ deep on the end before dropping deep. Is this where I start in the drop off area? No, because this type of area takes too long to cover with the baits I like to use.

I'm not setting up my usual test pattern casts, which may seem like I'm contradicting myself. I'm not, though, because time is a factor here. We may never get to fish this body of water again, so we have to make the best of the time we have.

If we assume that it's springtime here on Lake Gotta CatchUm, then this spot could be very good. I'll approach it with one bait— a top-water type of shallow bait.

What I'm trying to do is cover water. I'll position my boat where I can cast within 5´ of the bank with a controlled retrieve and still turn around in the boat and cast out over deeper water to pattern different depths. Pulling up shallow first accomplishes two things: it allows me to fish all the different levels of water that I feel are necessary, and in the case of clear lakes, it allows me to see the bottom to find out if it is *conducive to the fish*.

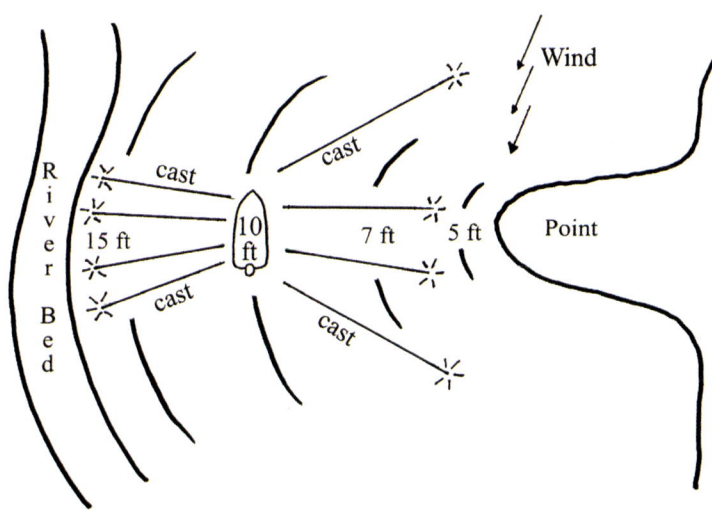

This version of Run-and-Gun casting is different than my usual test casting. I use this when I'm pressed for time, wanting to find spots more than just fish. Once I find my pattern spots, the following day I may go back to my usual test pattern. Notice how this hits many depths in a very short time.

If I pull up shallow and see the muck on the bottom that we never catch fish on, I probably won't make a cast. On the other hand, if I see the bottom is hard mud and gravel mixed with some cover and structure, I'll linger here for awhile because I've found a spot where fish *could* be. My baits should tell me if they're here.

To help move things along even faster, have the friend fishing in the boat with you throw shallow, then you throw deep. You cover more ground that way, or in this case, more water.

If you hang a fish over deep water, make some more casts to see if there are more fish in that area. Sometimes a school of smallmouth will be roaming this type of area. Pick them off before without spooking them. If no more fish appear to be in that spot, go to the spot immediately and check the depth. The fish was at that depth for a reason—not just for the heck of it. Don't venture too far from this point on either side. It's probably a waste of time, especially since you don't know the water on this new lake. This point is where I am trying to form my pattern.

Total time on this spot: Fifteen minutes.

Note: The points that I chose first will be on the side of the lake the wind could be blowing onto. This wind (if any) will determine my top water bait choice. More wind: chugger-type bait. Less wind: walking-bait, like a Spook.

My next choice would be to move to the secondary points back in bays or creeks off of the main channel. I'd repeat the same top-water process on these secondary points.

Total time: Fifteen minutes each.
(If you spend more than fifteen minutes on these spots, you've spent too much time.)

My next move on the new lake involves looking at the shoreline for those areas that are irregular in nature.

Example

I'm driving and looking at banks that have rock and gravel areas that all at once change to mud. I am going to assume, since I've never been here before, that this area could be good for the following reasons:

- It's spring, and the fish should be moving up to spawn.

- The crawfish that went into the mud last fall should be coming out of the same place.
- This spot is irregular in nature.

Spring, food source, and an irregular bottom configuration are all right here—three very good odds to help us narrow down a good House in our new lake.

Now I want to try to find some sort of pattern in this transition area I'm fishing. In most cases, fishermen will do one of two things. They start fishing by the transition area too fast, or sometimes they will parallel the bank and cover only certain depths. Both are okay test patterns, but not for this situation. I have a different way to address this site.

If there is a change on the bank, then I have to assume the transition at water level extends out into the water. I want to fish the exact transition. In other words, I want to fish right on top of it. By placing my boat just inside casting distance from the boat to the top of the transition spot, I can make my cast to the exact spot every time.

After several test casts, I move my boat and work my way out to deeper water. I am assuming (guessing) that the transition extends straight out into the water. I will then fish with the topwater bait or my trusted and loved grub exactly over the transition on every cast.

I'll keep moving out until I get to 10' to 12' of water. Then I'll move my boat to where my baits were hitting and repeat the process, moving back toward the bank. By placing my boat in this position and moving in, I've found out two things I need to know on this new lake: (if I catch a fish) the fish are here and what depth they are in.

Total time: 30 minutes with two people

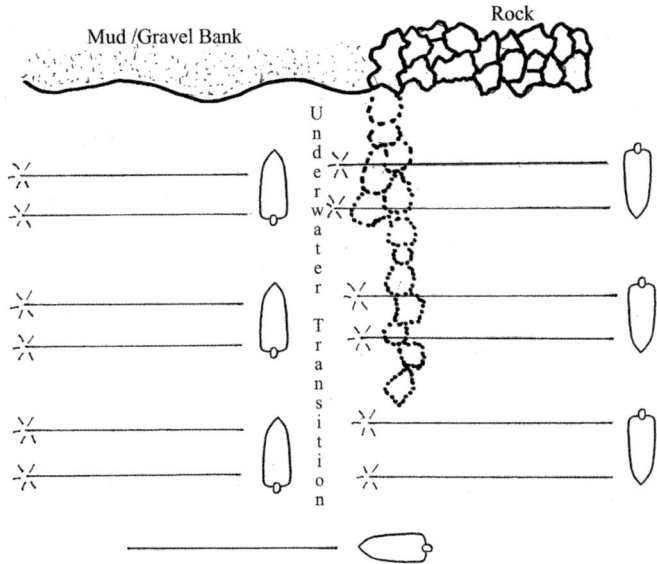

This Run-and-Gun test pattern is clearly different than my "known lake" pattern of fishing. It allows me to target the transition at all depths, then allows me to test the gravelly bottom I always love. Again, once I find my pattern on day one, tomorrow I might regroup and fish this with the test patterns I usually use.

My next move on this new lake is to a flat that looks promising. I'll approach this flat in very much the same way as the points we started on. If there are two people in the boat, we can hit these places hard and fast.

When I approach, I position my boat over 8' of water. I don't care if that 8' is 100 yards off the bank or 50. In most cases, the flat should have 8' of water about 40 yards from shore with 15' of water 40 or 50 yards on the other side of the boat.

In this case, I ride my trolling motor very little. I just want to stay in the same spot. On terribly windy days, I've been known to use an anchor. When anchored, I can focus my attention on every cast and not constantly fight the wind and trolling motor.

The idea of this *Run-and-Gun Pattern* is to very thoroughly fish the area with the circle. Think about how much of this one spot you're fishing. If you can cast 120' in one direction and your fishing partner is casting the same in another direction, you're covering an area of 80 yards.

Total time: thirty minutes (sometimes even less).

> **Note:** *I like to know if the water table is dropping or rising, but I rarely change my starting test depths. Under extreme conditions of rise, I might ease into slightly deeper depths, but only after testing my usual depth constants. Under falling conditions, I only fish harder. Dropping is a difficult condition to outsmart. I don't believe the fish follow the exact movements of a lake rise or fall, instead they back off of aggressive feeding habits and hang close to the House.*

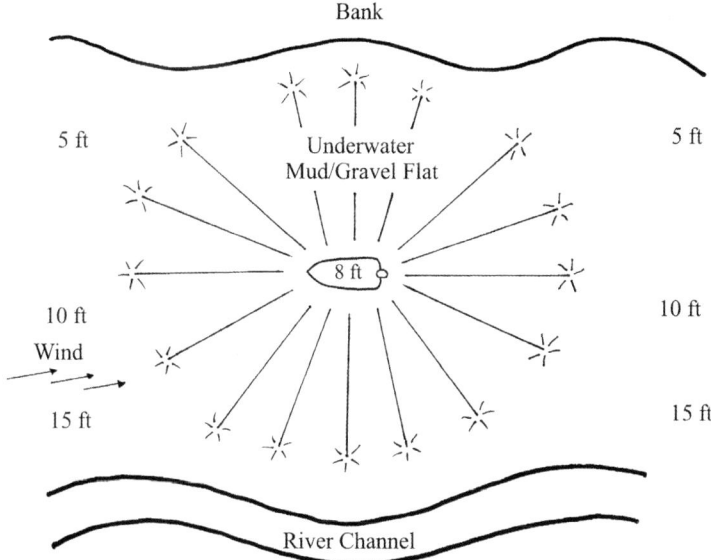

This Run-and-Gun test casting method can cover 80 yards of water in a very short period of time.

With the fan casting technique, my choice of baits has changed. Instead of using the top-water baits I used in the transition areas, on these long flats I like to use the grub in a chartreuse color. The reason for chartreuse is that I want the fish to be able to see it easily. Chartreuse does this well.

There is only one size lead head I use in this situation—the big round head 1/4 oz. The round head casts well in the wind with long distance, and I'm able to fish it a little faster because of the weight. I know that some of you are thinking about what I said earlier in the book about lead head sizes. Yeah, I usually like a 1/8 or 3/16 ounce in water that is shallow to 8'. In this situation, though, I'm not only fishing toward the bank to shallower water, I am also throwing the bait into deeper water. In both cases, I'm still able to control the bait. Even if I catch a fish, I'll more than likely stay with the 1/4 ounce because I'm still trying to form my pattern.

One Fish Does Not a Pattern Make

When forming a pattern, time is your enemy on a new lake. Why would time be your enemy—you've got three days to fish, right? The answer is both yes and no.

Remember that this is still springtime fishing. Fish, even in the spring spawn, go through different phases as the day progresses. In the early morning hours, the fish are active. As the day progresses, they get closer to home. Their bite has slowed a little, too. You have three days to fish, but you still only have peak hours on those three days. I'd much rather catch fewer fish in several places than to put all my eggs in one basket.

Keep in mind that if you fish one spot for three hours and catch five bass, you've got some fish, but you haven't learned a single thing about the rest of this lake. Even if you started at daylight, the bite might be calmed down by this time, and you'll have a much harder time forming patterns in other places. Your arch enemy, *Time*, has spanked you. When you're fishing an unfamiliar lake, persistence and patience are equally important. Stick to your guns and form that pattern. You'll have more information to use tomorrow.

Effectively, you've covered three different types of terrain (perhaps more than one of each), and you have used these three *Run-and-Gun Methods* of test casting. You've probably even caught fish in some of these places.

Here's a quick review of some smallmouth "givens" that we've probably proven with our *Run-and-Gun* technique.

1. A smallmouth bass is an open water, free roaming feeder but will never venture too far from home.
2. The best depths (in my opinion) for smallmouth bass are 8' to 15' of water. (You'll have tested this one thoroughly.)
3. Smallmouth bass like access to deep water.

With these factors in mind, I'll spend the next few hours roaming the spot where I caught the fish from the tests. I'll focus on access to deep water and the House where they live. Now, we'll fill in one more very important blank while forming our pattern: Is it cloudy or blue bird clear?

If it is cloudy, I'll concentrate my search in water 10' and shallower. If the sky is clear (high pressure), I'll spend my time focusing on 10' or more, looking for deep water access.

Now we're at mid day—the time all fisherman dread because they feel the fishing is over until the late afternoon comes. That's not necessarily true. When this time comes, I lay down my topwater bait entirely and concentrate on the grub and bottom-working baits like the tube or fly and pork frog. My *presentation* comes into play in a big way here. I'll offer these baits slow and easy. If I feel that the areas where I caught fish will hold fish tight to the House, I'll start my casts right there over the House, thinking back on places with deep water access. If I'm catching fish with this method, then this will be my pattern until the late afternoon hours tell me to pick up the top-water and add it back into my test.

It's absolutely imperative that you do not get in a hurry and start throwing crank baits and moving them so fast a fish couldn't catch one if he was swimming at top speed. You and I have probably found our pattern by now—use it. There is no doubt in my mind that everyone reading these pages has formed a pattern— *you* knowing that you've formed a pattern is the key.

Summertime Pattern *(Same unfamiliar lake)*

The heat of the summer changes the smallmouth game. To me, fishing is either shallow or deep—there's no middle ground. Smallmouth bass love cooler water. They're more active in 65° water than they'll ever be in 80° water. This is both a help and a hindrance to the fisherman because the criteria for finding House has just become more complicated. We have to try to find cooler water that is still capable of being a smallmouth home.

I'll leave the dock in the summertime with two baits tied on—a top-water and a bottom-working bait.

The first top-water bait I'll choose will be the Zara Spook (surprise, surprise) or maybe even the top-water grub. The Spook will create a commotion, where the grub will be much quieter, but still displace a small amount of water. If the fish are easily spooked, the grub will be a better choice. The Spook—well—it'll spook 'em. The bottom-working bait I have tied on will probably be a tube or fly and pork frog.

Here is how I approach each of them.

I will be concentrating most of my time on first and secondary points. Those seem to produce. Any time of year, I like to fish points, but they are a mainstay for me when the temperature is up.

Time spent casting in the summer is so important that the pages of this book cannot fully express it. I've found that only a few casts with a big top-water bait is enough for each spot, and then I move on. I may make no more than five casts with the Spook before I head for another point.

In the summertime, the fish on top of the point are looking for something to eat, and they become highly competitive. It's not unusual to pull up on a point and catch a smallmouth bass on the first cast, or at the very least get one to strike.

It's nearly impossible, though, to pull up on a point and catch a five-pound smallmouth bass, then catch another one on the same spot with more casts. Once I catch that big fish, I might make one or even two more casts, but then I'm gone looking for another point.

One reason for this, in my opinion, is that the big fish get the most food and they're usually alone. How many times have you taken the last piece of cake and eaten it real fast so no one would know? I've done it, and so has my brother, Randy ... a lot! It's survival of the fittest!

Unfortunately, now I've hung that fish in the shallow water of the point, and the commotion has spooked the other fish. They may come back, but I don't have time to wait—the sun is rising.

I head for another point and try to do the same thing there. If I see a spot like a big flat that I think could hold fish, I may stop and fish the spot with a few casts—but again, not many. Many fisherman, and I'm lumping myself in here too, pull up onto a flat and think they need to fish every inch of it. This is not a good practice. It wastes too much time when you fish such a big area. Remember, the sun is rising and the bass are heading home.

To make it short and sweet, I stay with the points on a new lake. If it is a northern, grass-filled lake, I find a point of grass. To make it even better, I look for a grass point that might hold different types of grass on the same point. (Irregular in nature).

Once the sun has hit the water for three hours, it will have warmed that shallow water even more. If I keep throwing the top water and nothing else, I feel like I am beating a dead horse. It's time to go deep and slow.

The deep and slow part could be on the ends of the points that I fished earlier.

> **Note:** *I may stay with the top-water bait longer if the weather is cloudy, and I know a low pressure area is moving in. I'll know the weather forecast before I head to the lake, whether it's new to me or one I've fished a thousand times. Do this for good fishing and for safety's sake, too.*

When I go to the bottom-working bait, it will be heavy enough that I won't lose contact with the bottom. If I'm in deeper water (and I will be), my choice of weight will be 1/4 ounce on the fly or the tube. Complete bottom contact is a must for me in this summertime test pattern.

The summertime pattern I use is short and sweet, but there's another summer thought I'd like to talk about. One more form of structure I use mid-day in the summertime test is *Humps*. When smallmouth bass are over the spawn, and their post-spawn activities are over as well, they tend to become loners again. They will, however, share their good spots with other smallmouth of the same general size. *Humps* in the lake are where this sharing takes place.

If I have a contour map of the new lake (a must), I'll look for these humps that may exist in the lake. I've been on very few lakes that did not have a few humps scattered out in the main body where you couldn't necessarily see them with the naked eye.

My bait choice doesn't change from that of the points, but it is time to break out the marker buoys. It is nearly impossible to tell where a smallmouth bass will be on a hump, because the wind and waves have very little to do with their positioning on that spot. It becomes hide and seek for the fisherman. I will also look for humps where the top of the hump is no shallower than 15' and down to 25'. This fishing situation *really* goes back to one of the four P's—*Patience*.

Can I tell you anything else about fishing a hump? Not really. It's up to you. It's even hard to tell exactly where the fish is on a hump. You just have to hope that he's there. In this situation, he probably will be. I'll go so far as to say that there are most likely many more fish on this particular piece of structure at this time of the year.

Humps may not be my first choice for the kind of structure I'd like to fish, but it is one I depend on in the summer. Do not forget your marker buoys. Catch one fish, toss a marker. Catch another, toss another marker. Then focus on those areas and the transition between them. Those buoys will be the focal point for your *Presentation*.

Winter/Fall Patterns (Same unfamiliar lake)

Cool weather brings on the bass and the fishermen—including me again with my top-water bait and grub. Fact is, there are several baits I use for this time of the year (meaning late September to December). Smallmouth bass have only one thing on their minds at this time—food, but their primary objective changes from crawfish to shad.

Lots of people know that large schools of shad will attract fish. This is a fact. Yet for me, the isolated shad patches mean more to me than the large schools. These small groups of baitfish roaming the banks can often have big smallmouth bass trailing behind or just under them—positioned to dash up or into them for an easy meal.

This is also the time that the smallmouth bass leave the deeper water like the humps. They move back a little shallower where we can find them a little easier.

I'll *never* leave the dock at this time of the year without a top-water bait tied on. My choice of top-waters does change from the Spook that makes the nice quiet wave on the surface to the noisy chugger type like the Tiny Torpedo or the Pop R series of baits. The grub will be a 3-1/2" chartreuse or white most of the time. There are exceptions, of course, but these two do produce.

I won't exclude the deep-water access spots I find on this new lake. There can and will be fish there. I'd just rather let Mother Nature dictate where I fish at this time of the year. By this, I mean the warmer water I find may be my starting point.

Example

I have two good prospects on this new lake. They both have the same characteristics. They're both on the southwest side of the lake with the same water clarity and depth, yet one bank holds 60° water while the other holds at 55°. I don't want to ignore the 55° water, but the 60° will be my first choice.

To take this example further, if the 60° water holds no visible baitfish, and the 55° water does, I'll start with the 55° to try and form a pattern. If in that 55° water the wind is hitting the bank, all the better. I know a north wind is not all that good sometimes, but in this case it can be.

The southwest side of the lake is not the only place that will hold fish, they could be anywhere. This goes back to the way I listen to my common sense and let it tell me where to go. You'll have the same intuition if you just put a few facts together.

To add to this pattern, I don't want the banks with the bolder-sized rocks, I'd rather have the mud and gravel we looked for in the springtime. Bass are smart enough to know there may be a few last-minute crawfish there heading in for the winter.

Another thing that's to our advantage in the wintertime is we don't have to worry so much about spooking the fish. It's harder to spook smallmouth in the wintertime. They're feeding and bulking up for the winter, so food is much more important than being scared. Also, they travel in packs at this time of year more than any other, so be ready. Once I catch that big fish, I cast for another.

I also watch to see if the visible baitfish move. If they do, so do the fish. If I can see the baitfish on the surface, I'll move with them as long as it is practical. Also in this case—and this is very important—*if you are following the baitfish, do not throw into them!* Baitfish spook just like bass. Make those casts to the rear. This way, you won't spook the baitfish and you may pick up the bass following close behind. One exception to that rule would be if a fish comes up in the middle of the baitfish—then, I'm going to throw at it.

Catching bass in the cold months is as much a matter of common sense as it is using testing patterns. Use your pattern and remember that *water + food = bass*. Take what you know and what you've read in this book and have a great time on a new lake.

Use what you learned when you get home … you might be surprised!

Catch 'em when you find 'em.

CHAPTER TWENTY-TWO

Flashers and Graphs

When I go back and think about the many days I've spent on the water chasing smallmouth bass, I think about how important the flashers and graphs were to me in my quests. I guess you could say that my fishing success increased as the electronics grew in style and performance. Good electronics will aid you with finding fish and also help you determine which fish are catchable.

It's not imperative that you own the best of the best when it comes to using technology, but it's obvious that each improvement in these devices will help you catch fish. The graph or sonar you choose to purchase is up to you. To help you with your decision, I will try to describe how electronics have changed over the years and what I did with these new marvels to expand my fishing.

There are several things I want my flasher or graph to do, including:

- indicate how deep my boat is sitting,

- show anything irregular in nature below me (hump, drop off, rock ridge, etc.), and
- indicate what form of wood cover there is (stumps, fallen trees, brush etc.).

When any two of these factors come together, I may have found the spot, but there is more research to do before this spot goes into my records.

When I first started guiding in the '70s, all I had was a flasher. I used it to tell me where I was in relation to where I wanted to have my boat positioned. I wanted more, but that was about all they would do then. You have to remember that electronics were still in their infancy, but they did serve their purpose.

As time went on, I was lucky enough to get a little attention in the fishing industry and had the advantage of sponsored boats. These boats were rigged the way I wanted them and had much better flashers. At this point, I had two on my boat instead of just

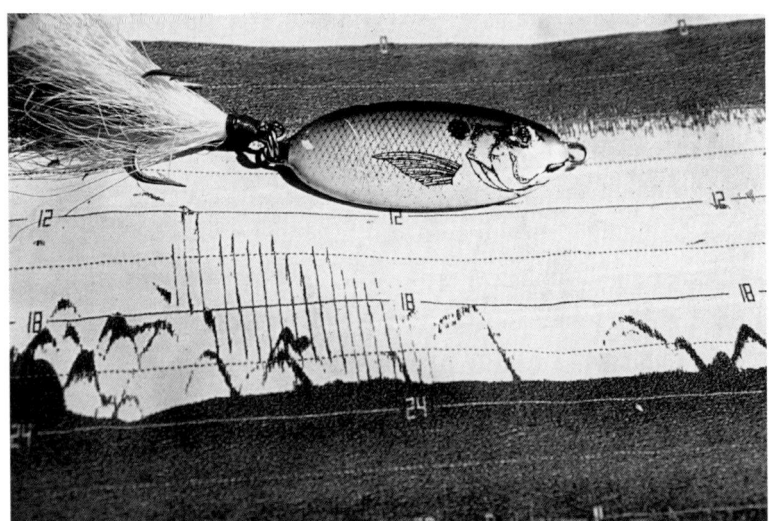

These characteristic arcs on the early graphs designate fish that are feeding and catchable.

one, and I also had my first graph. This technology was new and had a roll of paper that was loaded on a spool and placed inside the machine. When the unit was turned on, a stylist would mark the paper as it turned. This was very good, because it would not only mark the bottom, it also marked the fish as inverted Vs. This was truly amazing to me!

At first I used this technology most when I was striper fishing. I'd mark the fish, drop the bait to the exact depth, and hang on. This was when I started thinking that exact depth fishing could apply to smallmouth bass like it did with stripers. It did, and a new world of fishing opened up for me (and many other fishermen).

The most important part of this new graph was its ability to locate irregular features on the bottom. Fish gravitate to these areas, so the better I lined up on them, the more productive my fishing was. It's easy to *see* the brush pile sticking up out of the water, but place that same brush in 20 feet of water and it becomes a little more difficult.

The graph showed me the features of the bottom and, if the sensitivities were set correctly, I would know if it was a hard or soft bottom. The softer bottoms were displayed by the graph as a much fatter line. When the thickness of this bottom line changed, I could assume that there was a transition, and I'd focus on fishing that area. If the fish were at a certain depth near these transitions, I would try to work my bait at that depth. It took time to learn to work certain baits and certain depths, but some great fishing systems emerged from those early years of finally seeing those fish on the graph and being able to target them strategically.

Electronics help you to become a better fish finder — the devices even became known as *fish finders*. Remember, you can't catch fish until you find them, and finding is the first and most important stage of fishing.

So, what do you look for on these newer graphs? It's easy to get caught up in everything your graph and flasher graphics show you. There is an overwhelming abundance of information available on these machines, but it's useless until you know what you're looking at on the screen.

I learned the hard way that too much information with no knowledge of how to use it is the same as not having any information at all. In order to make electronics work for you, first you must determine what you need to know. Let's make a short list that deals with fish, especially smallmouth bass:

1) Smallmouth favor deeper water and consider that deeper water cover.

2) Smallmouth like irregular spots in nature—humps, drops, anything that changes the bottom features quickly.

3) Smallmouth will use brush, especially stumps, as home, and the stumps will be in deeper water.

4) Smallmouth bass use grass lines under the water. You will need to know what they look like on the machine you're using.

For me, fishing these isolated pieces of cover and structure has become the biggest factor in finding and catching big smallmouth bass. It's kind of like having the house on the hill overlooking the subdivision below. The subdivision may be nice but that beautiful house on the hill is a sanctuary, so to speak, for Mr. Big (the bigger fish). The same holds true for the field of stumps all bunched together on a point. These stumps might be a good place to fish, but the three stumps 30 yards from the rest is the ideal location.

There are two main reasons for this, and why I search so hard to find these special locations. The first reason is that the big bass like these areas (proven fact), and the second — and most important — is that maybe no one else has found this spot. Finding those special isolated spots will help you zero-in on the bigger and better fish. Every smallmouth is a good one (yeah, I'm prejudiced), but those big-uns are what keep us bass boys beating the water to a froth.

I know this question comes to your mind, as it did to mine a long time ago: If I can't see the cover, how do I know what I'm looking at?

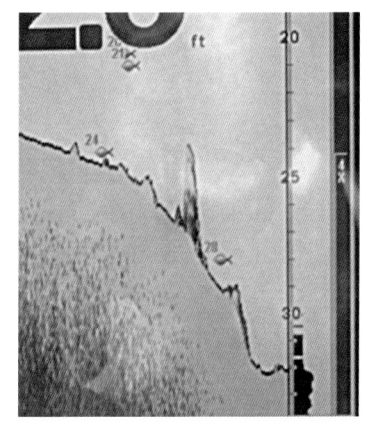

With the electronics we have today, the depth range can be set so that you can find stumps in 8 feet of clear water—run over them, and see what they look like on the screen. After a little work, you move out deeper and try to find the same thing using what you learned at the shallow depth. Basically the spots will look the same, but you may notice more fish on one or the other. It's really hard to know which fish will bite when viewing them on a screen, but approaching each spot systematically will teach you which fish on those spots will hit a bait.

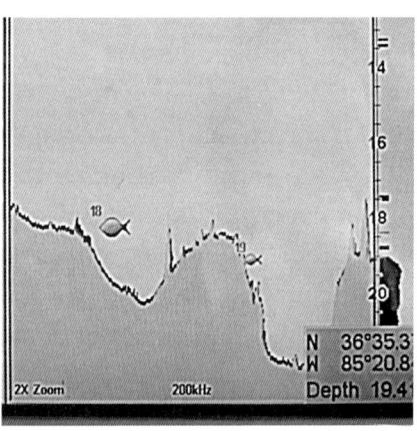

Fish holding tight to structure will need slower action from your lure, but are more likely to bite than the scattered and suspended fish.

The new graphs on the market now show fish everywhere (every little fish fart is detected), which makes it easy to throw at everything you see. Try to narrow these special spots down systematically by truly testing each one. Remember what that graph showed you when you caught a fish, not just the pretty fish on the graph. Find, locate, and remember those good spots, and be sure to document why they are good.

Once you find the particular cover you want to test, throw a marker buoy and fish the area. Use the graph to *fish-find* and mark the spot with a buoy. So few fishermen properly use marker buoys. It's an age-old system that is deadly. Don't be fooled by thinking you can find the spot again from visuals or by using the graph. You were probably lucky to find it on the first pass and you'll miss it on the next! I'll say it again. Find the spot and mark it. Then fish it.

I always try to throw my marker on the up-wind side of the cover or structure. Doing so does not interfere with my cast when I stick my boat into the wind on the lower side of what I've found. It's terrible when the boat or bait gets caught up in the marker. Learn boat placement when setting the markers in the first place and it'll make your casts easier and more productive.

As my years of fishing progressed and the number of fishermen increased, the electronics became more and more important. The readouts nearly told you what kind of fish you were looking at, but not quite. Knowledge of the fish and its habits still came into play when looking at the screen, especially since the technology had progressed to the point that it could distinguish between different forms of cover. Because of this, fishermen started to fish in areas that had never seen an angler's bait. *The age of freshwater deep water fishing had begun.*

I'm not saying this was the first time a fisherman had fished in deep open water cover and structure, but with this technology the fisherman had a much better grasp of the environment the fish live in, therefore his fishing success increased fivefold. No longer did he have to line up behind other boats on a bank and throw at a fish that had been dodging crank baits all day long. He now had a choice. As I so often say, "If you can hit the bank with a bait, 90% percent of the fish in the lake are on the other side of the boat." The other side of the boat calls for electronics.

Earlier I said that our old paper graphs marked fish with

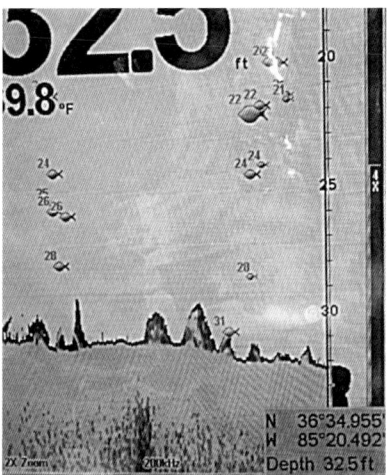

Suspended fish are always difficult to catch. I would focus on the big one hugging the stump on the bottom.

inverted Vs. Now, they mark them with little fish symbols. That's cool. I think this mark makes the fisherman more aware of what may be down there, and most definitely makes the isolated pieces of cover and structure easier to stay on when you see little fish on the screen. When they start coloring them brown or green for me, I'll get even more excited!

Don't be fooled into thinking that you have to mark tons of fish on the screen in order to fish a good spot. Remember that good spots hold good fish … not necessarily volumes of fish. Sometimes, three fish on two tight stumps in the perfect water will be more than enough to make you a happy angler.

When you find these special spots with three or four fish hanging on them, pay very close attention to the position of the fish on the cover. If the target is brush cover for example, and the fish are tight to the brush, a slow bait presentation will be called for. If the fish are venturing out farther from the brush, then a faster presentation could be called for. Unfortunately, you only have one chance at viewing this show on your screen because you don't want to run back over the spot after you've thrown the buoy. Make your markers count and keep a very close eye on the information you see. One pass is probably all you have.

On a recent mid-September trip to Dale Hollow Lake, Darren (my co-author) asked me to take a good friend of his, Dale Rogers, out on the lake for a little fishing. It was a perfect day — north wind, 90 degrees, clear water, and bluebird high pressure — a great day for bowling. Nevertheless, we left the dock and my years of fishing experience started rolling around in my brain. I couldn't rely on luck today; I had to test my textbook theories and approach this thing systematically (like I keep telling Darren).

On this day there were no visible baitfish on the graph, the water was 80 degrees, and it was the middle of the day with the sun hitting hard. Banks were out of the question — a waste of time — hence the electronics. I know Dale thought it was strange that I never got the boat on plane. We just kept talking and I kept watching the screen. I felt that 15 feet of water or more would be our target area if we expected to catch some fish or at least stand a shot at catching some.

After about 30 minutes of motoring around, I started to mark a very irregular bottom. I grabbed a marker buoy and within a few minutes I saw something that looked promising sticking up from the bottom — large brush pile or an old tree with four very good fish marks. I threw the buoy in 26 feet and we began to fish.

To shorten this story, we hung three fish — one, a five-pound-plus smallmouth. We were 150 yards from the closest bank on one piece of cover. Before we left and after we picked up our buoy, we went over the spot, and one fish remained in the cover.

We'd hooked all but one of the fish on that spot. Even though we'd released the fish, we'd spooked them and only one of our group was left on the spot. This was the perfect situation — we'd been able to locate, mark, and pick them off like rubber duckies at the county fair.

So, I'll bet you're wondering how much electronics a fisherman needs, and how to choose between the many on the market? Tough questions, here's what I look for when purchasing a graph.

• A good sized screen where I don't have to squint to see what it's showing me.

• A detailed readout, in other words I want the image I see to look like what it is — fish, brush, treetop, etc.

• A color screen is a big advantage too, because it gives you more information.

• A good zoom option so that if I move to shallower water I can set the depth so I still have a full screen readout. (The same holds true if I move deeper.)

Buying a graph (LED) readout is like buying a television — some are just sharper than others. Ask around, talk with your buddies to see what they have to say. Electronics won't make you a better fisherman — but they will make you a more successful fisherman. The rest is up to you.

"Catch 'em when you find 'em," document your catch, and remember what that screen looked like — if you caught fish you'll be looking for more places just like that one!

*If you can't feel the bait,
you will never feel the fish when it hits.*

CHAPTER TWENTY-THREE

A Nearly-Forgotten Article

The following Article was published in Bassmaster Magazine *November 1988. We would like to offer special thanks to our friends at* **Bassmaster** *for allowing us to share this with fishermen in book form. Valuable lessons are learned when great minds think alike. ~DS*

The Great Smallmouth Hunt

To find smallmouth on an unfamiliar lake, first find the pattern ...

TONY BEAN 1988

Maybe you've been there before: After trying every lure in your tackle-box and exhausting every hole you've ever caught a fish from (and a few new ones, as well), you return to the marina to moan about the poor fishing with the other unfortunate souls.

Then, just as you all arrive at the conclusion that it was just not meant to be, a spoiler shows up with a huge stringer of small mouth bass.

What happened? Was it luck?

More than likely, luck had very little to do with the angler's success. His secret, odds are, was in forming a *pattern* for catching bass.

What is a pattern? A pattern is a set of circumstances or conditions under which a fish will be enticed to feed. And they can change from day to day as the weather and water conditions and lake levels change.

Patterns are discovered through a process of elimination. The angler who rules out unproductive conditions and circumstances quickest will find the right combination before anyone else. And the one who fails to establish a productive pattern must depend purely on luck to catch bass. This is especially true with smallmouth bass, I have found in my years of guiding for bronze-backs on Percy Priest Reservoir and other Tennessee lakes.

Still, some fishermen hold the view that the answer to catching a limit of small mouths is in finding a particular spot where the bass are abundant. The place is not as important as the combination of depth, cover and structure, water temperature and other environmental factors occurring in that spot. Find other spots with similar conditions, and you should find bass.

It should also be understood that more' than one pattern can payoff in bass at the same time.

Testing The Theory

To demonstrate the importance of a pattern and to test the theory that more than one pattern under the same conditions can produce fish, I decided to conduct an experiment.

I asked three of my acquaintances from three different states — all experienced and successful smallmouth fishermen — to join me on a lake none of them had ever fished. Their assignment was to form a pattern to catch smallmouth bass and to make note of the processes they used to arrive at their patterns. Naturally, the success of the pattern each one selected would be measured by the number and size of the fish each caught.

The lake I selected was Woods Reservoir in Middle Tennessee. This 4,000-acre impoundment is well-known for its trophy smallmouth, and it is where I learned to bass fish when I was a boy.

The three participants in this experiment were Jack Christian, an experienced small mouth guide on Percy Priest Lake in Nashville, Tenn.; Brad Weakley, a smallmouth guide from Shepardsville, Ky.; and Steve Bernstein, an experienced and successful smallmouth angler from St. Louis, Mo.

It was early November, and the fishing conditions were what most anglers expect — and dread — at this time of year: northeast winds, a temperature fluctuation of 40 degrees within the previous two days, high atmospheric pressure and bluebird skies.

Earlier that same week, Middle Tennessee had experienced temperatures ranging from the mid-80s during the day to the lower 50s at night. That was pretty reasonable for November in Tennessee, but when the three anglers arrived at Morris Ferry dock at 5:30 a.m. on Friday, the thermometer at the marina showed a brisk 29°, and the high was predicted to go only into the low 50s.

In addition, the reservoir itself had been drawn down to perhaps its lowest level since it was built. The drawdown confused the fish and a lot of local fishermen as well.

I couldn't have asked for better, or maybe I should say tougher conditions to prove the importance of finding a pattern. The conditions were tough and the three anglers were going to have to use their heads if any fish were to be caught on this day.

Connell Norton and Della Gates, owners of Morris Ferry Dock., assured our group that the fish had been hitting all week and a number of good-sized smallmouth bass had been brought in. Still, the group looked less than confident. The immediate concern seemed to be the effect of the cold front on the bass.

Preliminary Strategies

As each angler readied his equipment and prepared to launch his boat, I asked each to describe his strategy.

"I'm going to tie on two medium-running crank baits, a shad color and a crawfish color," said Steve Bernstein. "If I am able to establish a pattern with crank baits this morning, I believe it will probably hold for the next two days.

"Normally, the crank bait in either shad or some form of crawfish color is a good producer this time of the year. Crawfish take on different colors during different times of the year and in different reservoirs. In fact, my favorite crawfish color in one lake may not work at all in another.

"I don't believe it's necessary for the bait to look exactly like a crawfish, but I do believe the color is extremely important. I prefer solid colors in different shades over the exact imitation.

"But I have my doubts as to whether they will be effective during this cold front," he added. "Cold fronts normally send fish deep, especially smallmouth. But since I am unfamiliar with the lake, I'm going to start with the crank baits anyway."

Brad Weakley, a top guide on Kentucky's Taylorsville Lake, was tying on crank baits, too, but he had also added 1/4-ounce black hair jigs to two more of his rods.

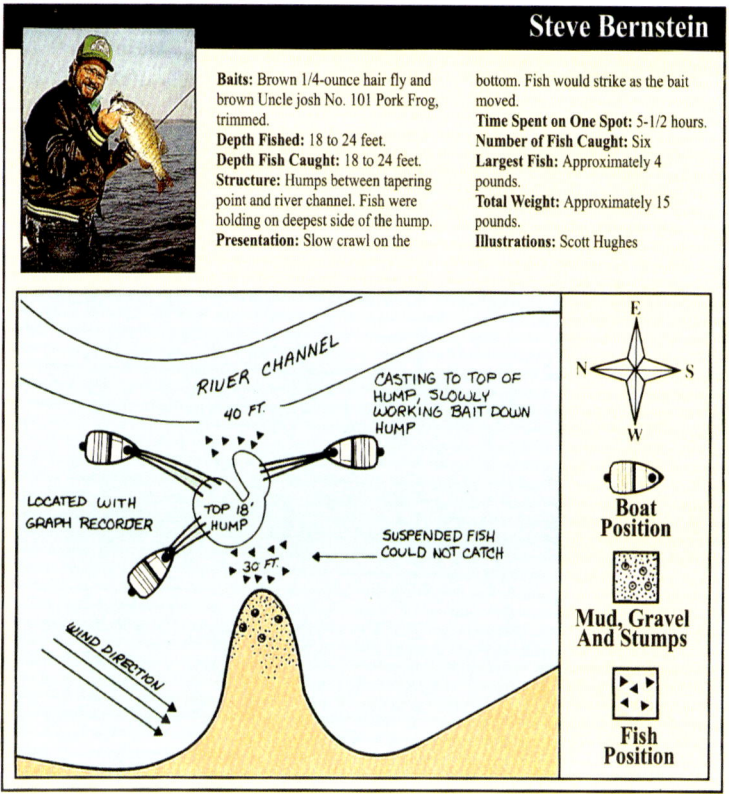

"I'm going to start on points that look like they would hold smallmouth and work my way in while using the 'fly' and (pork) chunk," he explained. "Then I'll switch to a medium-to-deep-running crank bait as soon as the water is shallow enough for me to work the crank bait close to the bottom.

"Both baits are excellent bass producers and I've noticed that there are shad everywhere. Yet I have a feeling that shad won't be what the fish are feeding on this morning. The bass are apt to stay deeper and go for an easier meal of crawfish rather than chasing the shad. That's what they usually do during a cold front."

Jack Christian, the small mouth and striper guide, stood on the bank and watched shad flicking on the surface.

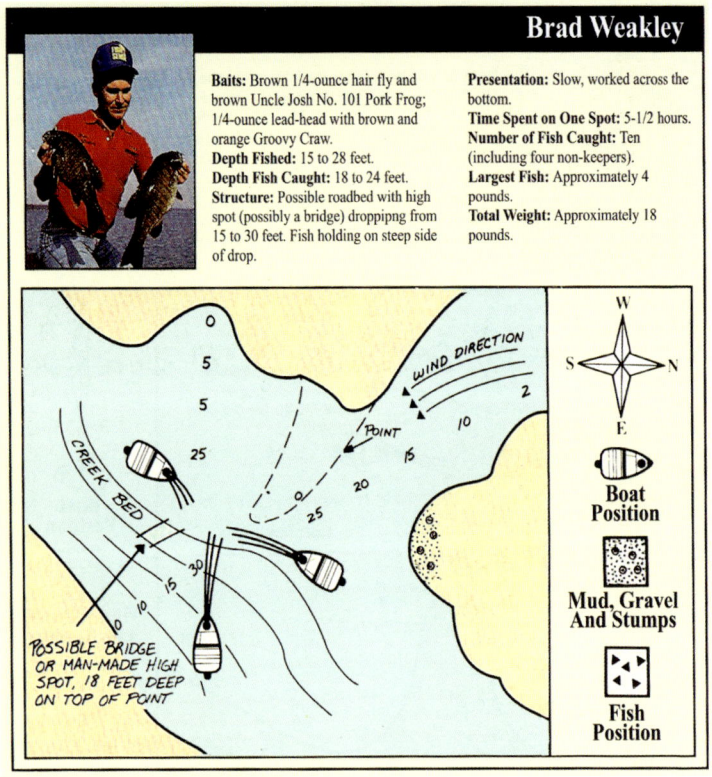

"There's a lot more bait activity than I thought there would be after this temperature drop," he said. "Maybe the shad will be just what we need. I guess I'll start with the shad-colored crank baits. The pattern will be faster to form if that's what they're after.

"But the cold front may have changed that. While they're hard to ignore, I don't want the abundance of shad to dictate my whole day of fishing."

As they left the ramp at 6:30 a.m. each angler headed for the lower end of the lake. They had studied maps of the lake and had asked questions about typical smallmouth habits there, and each had decided that the lower end of Woods would be more productive.

Asking Questions

Tom Orr, my fishing partner from Nashville, and I headed for the marina where Della had a hot pot of coffee brewing and ham and eggs on the stove.

As we finished our breakfast, I asked Tom Tilley, an OMC salesman from Manchester, Tenn., and a frequent angler on Woods, to size up the day's fishing.

He and Larry Schrader of Chattanooga had fished all night.

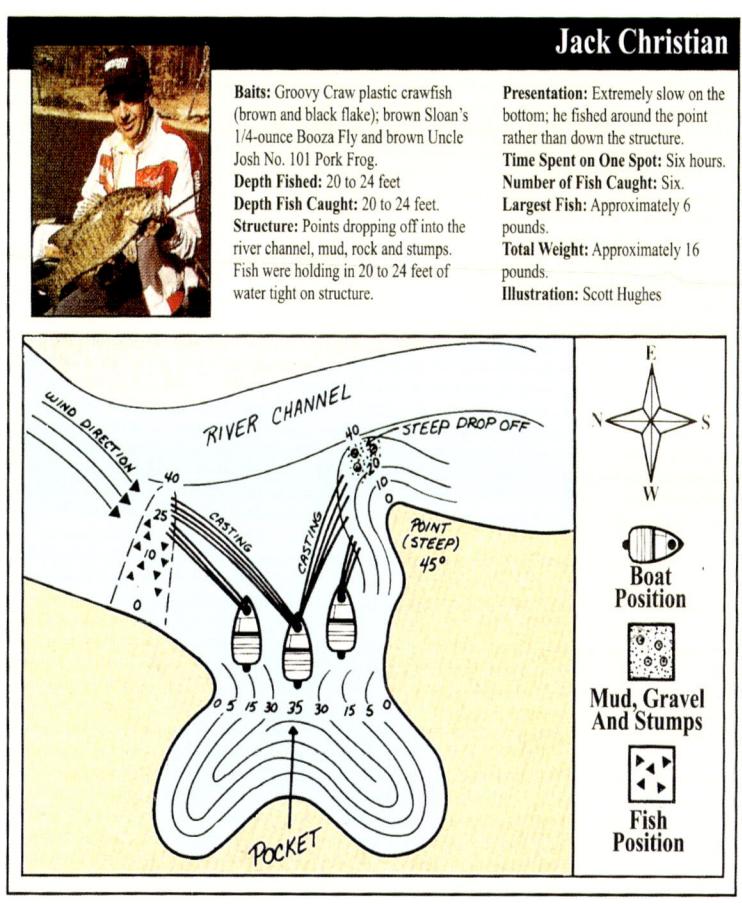

"We caught several good bass last night, including two over 3 pounds," Tilley said. "But we started before the cold front settled in, and the fish were turned on.

"Most of our fish came from 6´ to 15´ of water, which is not unusual at this time of year. Fishing isn't that bad, but it's probably better at night than during the day.

"Right now the weather is really affecting the fish, so the choice of baits will be critical to forming a pattern. The bass should be in 15´ of water or deeper, and a slow-working bait in a crawfish color should work best. "

He predicted that my smallmouth experts would find bass in deep water close to steep drop-offs, and that they would have better success on a small hair jig with a No. 101 Uncle Josh pork frog or a crank bait like a Rapala Fat Rap or a Rebel Deep Wee R.

Larry Schrader also suggested that a short-arm spinner bait tipped with a pork-rind trailer would attract bass around drop-offs deeper than 15´.

"Putting a pattern to these fish is going to be tough. Woods can be difficult to catch fish on, even when you know the pattern," he added.

How do those approaches compare to the ones selected by our smallmouth experts?

Both Bernstein and Weakley had tied on crawfish-colored crank baits and the fly-and-pork chunk. Christian figured shad-colored baits would be the answer. And all three planned to fish points instead of the steep drop-offs Tilley and Schrader thought would be the best structure.

Early-Morning Efforts

9:30 a.m. — Three hours had passed and it was time to check on our fishermen. Tom Orr and I found Steve Bernstein in open water, more than 100 yards from the bank. He summarized his first few hours of fishing.

"I started out on points, working from places with big rocks toward gravel. I worked the crank baits in both shad and crawfish colors from the bank out to about 15´. The only takers were small largemouth, all on the crawfish color. It seems funny that they would want the crawfish color with all those shad working the surface, but that appears to be the case.

"I decided that under the current conditions, a smallmouth pattern can't be formed in close to the bank on crank baits, so I started looking for some form of structure off the bank with my graph. I think I've figured out where the fish are. Now it's just a matter of figuring out what they want."

10:30 a.m. — By this time, Brad Weakley had given up on the crank baits as well, and he had changed colors of the fly and pork chunk.

"I believe the fish have moved off of the banks and back into deeper water," he said. "Crank baits may catch a few fish today, but the bigger fish — smallmouth in particular — have gone deeper."

He was fishing over a high spot on the bottom that he had guessed to be a bridge on an old roadbed. The high spot was 15´ deep, dropping into 30´ of water.

"The fish are using the edge of the drop, so I am working the fly and chunk down the drop from 15´ to 18´," he said. "The majority of strikes — and they are few and very light — are coming in about 18´ to 24´ of water. I really have to be alert and set the hook immediately. The bass are not holding onto the bait very long. If they are, it's hard to feel that initial strike."

Jack Christian was fishing closer to a bank, but the bank was not a significant part of his pattern.

"I moved into this pocket because of the depth of water in here," he said. "It seemed to be a good spot to work a wide range of water depths and find out just what level the fish were holding.

"The crank bait did not produce, so I've been using a fly-and-rind and a rubber crawfish on a 1/4-ounce lead-head. I nearly had my rod snatched away from me just a short while ago. The fish hit the rubber craw while I was working it slowly on a point on this river channel in about 20´ of water. I think the key to today's pattern will be a bait that has to be worked very slowly."

I watched as Christian worked his lure; it took about two minutes between casts. Now that's slow.

11 :00 a.m. — Bernstein was still on the same spot.

"I've found the hot spot, if there is one today," he said with a smile. "I had been fishing a point that drops into 30´ of water. As I began moving around it, I found a hump about 20´ deep that drops off into about 40´ of water. Looking at the map, I discovered that the 40´ drop is the river channel, and the hump is between the river channel and the end of the point."

Bernstein reached into his live well and pulled out a chunky 3-1/2 pound smallmouth.

"I've got three more - not that size but respectable 2-pounders. I caught them on a brown 1/4-ounce hair jig and brown No. 101 pork frog. I trimmed the fat off so the bait would fall quicker and have a little more action once it touched down on the bottom.

"They're not real aggressive, and it's hard to feel the hit," he added. "With this big fish, I only felt some resistance on the bait, sort of like a leaf feels when you get one caught on a crank bait. The fish seem to be holding just off to the side of the drop-off in about 20´ of water."

11:45 a.m. — Weakley had not moved. "These fish are driving me nuts!" he complained. "I know they're here, and I know they're not going anywhere. At most, they may move to slightly shallower water as the day progresses.

"I do have two 3 1/2-pound smallmouth but that's all for the moment. I'm using a 4″ worm on a hair jig and a hair jig with a No. 101 pork chunk. Brown seems to be the color of preference. If nothing happens in the next few minutes, I'll probably try a new location. But I do intend to stay with this depth and this bait. I feel it will produce if I can just find the right place."

Afternoon Action

12:15 p.m. — Christian was still on the same spot over the roadbed in 20′ of water.

"I've switched from 10-pound test line to 6-pound line for more distance in this deeper water, and I'm still using the rubber crawfish in brown with black flakes. I've got three small fish in the boat, but I think there's probably a bigger one down there."

Christian set the hook and brought a 2-pound smallmouth to the boat.

"If you don't set the hook immediately on these fish, you can forget it. They just are not as aggressive as smallmouth normally are. But they're here, and that's what counts.

"Crawfish are obviously the key to the pattern today and if the temperature continues to warm as it is doing, the fish should become more aggressive and fishing ought to pick up some."

I asked Christian if he thought that the fish would move shallower as the water warmed.

"Possibly tonight they will," he responded. "I don't believe I will try to fish any shallower. The pattern I have is catching fish, so I guess it makes sense to stay with it."

Bernstein was still fishing the same 2′ hump.

"These fish will hit, but they're slow. I'm going to stick with them right here—and then, right before dark, I'll move up a little shallower and see if the fish have moved up. I'm probably in a good spot and with only a few hours of light left it really doesn't make sense to start looking elsewhere. I did try a jigging spoon but didn't get a hit. What fish I am catching are on the fly, so I'll stay with it until I'm certain that I need to change."

1:30 p.m. — Weakley has moved to a new location.

"My fish seem to have quit or moved, so I thought I would try a new place. This point extends out and drops off into the river channel. So far I have only caught one fish, and it was small."

Weakley had added an orange and brown rubber crawfish to one of his rods.

"If crawfish are the key to the pattern, and I've about decided that they are, then I am going to try and imitate the craw. Since the fish will not chase a bait today and the hits are real light, then the Groovy Craw (a plastic crawfish made by Fishing Enterprises in Dickson, Tenn.) fished dead-slow on the bottom could do the trick."

2:20 ·p.m. — Christian still had not moved, but now he was smiling.

"I got it," he said as he reached into the live well. "A Woods Reservoir trophy smallmouth—about 6 pounds or more! I kept working the craw off the drop in about 20´ of water and the fish nailed it."

Since his main goal was to form a pattern for smallmouth, he had stayed over the structure longer than if he had been in a tournament, when every ounce counts.

"I probably would have moved had I been fishing a tournament," he said. "But then I wouldn't have this big fish.

"The key to these smallmouth today is to fish slowly and be patient. It's easy to fish one place a long time when the fish are hitting, but it's hard when they aren't aggressive."

That is especially so when you're fishing deep water. "For some reason, every fisherman prefers to find fish in shallow water," Christian suggested. "But for smallmouth, 20' is not really deep."

3:30 p.m. — I checked on Bernstein again.

"My fish have slacked off, but I have six keepers and I feel good about that," he said.

He confirmed the importance of persistence. "Any smallmouth lake can be tough; you just have to be patient and establish a pattern," Bernstein emphasized. "If I had run from place to place today, I would be lucky to have two good smallmouth. That's the problem with a lot of fishermen, myself included. Even though we catch some fish and form a pattern, sometimes we still don't recognize the pattern.

"For example, a fisherman stops and fishes a point and catches no fish. Then he fishes a flat and a pocket and catches no fish. Then he fishes a drop-off and catches fish. What does he look for next? Another drop-off? No, he stops on another point where he hasn't caught a fish all day. Forming a pattern is one thing—recognizing the pattern is something else."

Late Afternoon

4:00 p.m. — Weakley had returned to his original spot.

"The fish have slowed down, but I can't complain," he said. "I have six keepers and turned back four small ones. They want the rubber crawfish, but I didn't figure that out until it was really too late to score.

"I feel it's important to stay with a pattern until it's absolutely necessary to change. It's like a deer hunter climbing a tree before daylight. He's in a good tree, but as it gets lighter, he sees a tree that looks better, so he changes trees. And then he changes again and again until finally he looks back and sees a deer standing under the tree he started with. He should have stayed there, but by then it's too late."

4:30 p.m. — Christian was still on the same spot. "The fishing really hasn't picked up any in the afternoon like I thought it might, but I've got the fish that I wanted. I may have stayed on this spot too long, but I don't regret it.

"On a lake you fish frequently, it's not so bad to run to several different spots in hopes that the pattern you used last week will still be working. But when you establish a pattern on a lake you aren't familiar with, you had better stick with it as long as there's a possibility that fish can still be taken. They always say that patience is a virtue, but for a fisherman, patience is a must."

Quitting Time

At **5 p.m.**, everyone met in the middle of the lake and discussed the day's events. It had taken all three fishermen about three hours to get on the patterns, and they stayed with the patterns until the day was over. Each spent more than five hours fishing one spot — that, too, was part of their patterns.

They agreed that weather conditions (bluebird skies, high pressure and northeast winds) were very tough for smallmouth fishing, but lake conditions were good, even though the lake was extremely low. Water clarity ranged from semi-clear to stained in the lower end, and the water temperature was 59° at the surface.

The air temperature did warm some during the day but none of the fishermen felt that it had much effect on the smallmouth.

The choice of baits changed after about two hours into the morning. Crank baits were replaced with slower-working baits like the "fly-and-rind" and plastic crawfish — both designed to work deeper than crank baits.

What is more, all three fishermen independently arrived at these same conclusions:

- That the bass were holding in 16´ to 24´ of water on some form of drop, hump or steep bank, and always on the steepest part of the structure.
- That slow movement was the key to whatever bait was used.
- That bass wanted baits imitating crawfish, not baitfish.
- That fishing would be best on the lower end of the lake.

And all three agreed that establishing a pattern was paramount to success.

"I don't believe a person could have much chance of catching a stringer of fish here during this time of the year and under these conditions without forming some kind of a pattern and sticking with it," said Brad Weakley.

Steve Bernstein added, "Maybe there is a better daytime pattern than I found, but I'm pleased with what I did and I would probably do it the same way under the same conditions."

"This was not a tournament but a day for forming a pattern, so the pressure was off," said Jack Christian. "For me, this was just another day of fishing, so I could really concentrate on thoroughly working an area where I felt I had a better-than-average chance of catching something."

It is interesting to note that Tom Tilley and Larry Schrader had accurately predicted the pattern, including the productive baits and the best structure and depth range. Their analyses were based on their experience on the lake in various seasons and under all conditions. Each of the three experts involved in the pattern-finding exercise relied on a thorough knowledge of the smallmouth and an understanding of deep-water structure.

If nothing else, the experience at least should prove that a successful smallmouth angler doesn't count on luck, instead he relies on logic, knowledge, persistence and a great deal of patience. And, of course, a pattern. ~TB

Carl Haley shows a perfect lipping technique on this beautiful Percy Priest Smallmouth

*If you are following the baitfish,
do not throw into them!
Baitfish spook just like bass.*

CHAPTER TWENTY-FOUR

"The Last Chapter"

Throughout this book, cover to cover, I have tried to give you all of the information I can to help you understand what happens when you "put the puzzle together."

I want you to experience the same types of fishing thrills that I've had in my lifetime fighting what I consider to be the best game fish of them all.

After you've gone through the trial and error and educational process of learning good fishing techniques, I want you to have that feeling of coming out on top as you hold a five pound-plus smallmouth bass for the first time.

I want you to be able to take that five pounder, photograph and document it, then release it back into the water—because you now have confidence in yourself and in your fishing abilities and know you can go out and do it again.

Displaying a half-dozen smallmouth bass mounts on your office wall is impressive, but witnessing those big fish being released back into the wild to perhaps gain still another pound in their lifetime is even more thrilling—especially when you know you might catch that same fish again. That's just magnificent!

There's something else I hope to achieve for my angler friends, as well. I want you to take your kids and grandkids to the river, the creek, or the lake and show them what it's like to *learn* fishing. Don't just sit them in the back of the boat with nothing to do but text their buddies. Time spent on the water with kids *sounds like* it's all about them, but you'll find it's just as much about you.

I wouldn't take any amount of money for the times I've spent with my son on the waters of this United States. I remember the smiles and excitement on my son's face when he caught fish, but even more, I remember the smiles he wore when I asked him to come with me.

Jay is an excellent fisherman, and we've spent some wonderful times together. Now, he has the chance to take his son, Zachary, and do the same thing. As a grandparent, I have the opportunity to fish with my grandson. Zachary and I will share as many moments in the creeks and lakes as we can—and in him I will see the future of all kids who look forward to putting on their tennis shoes and heading for a creek to wade.

The young people we inspire to love fishing will be the sportsmen and sportswomen who carry the future torch for our American waterways. That's a big deal. Always remember this ... the size of the fish matters more to the parents than it does to the kids. They just want to be with us and learn the many wonders of life by our sides. Together we'll learn about fishing ... and life.

Of all the photos I've taken in my life, this is the one I've waited for. My grandson, Zachary Bean, had a great morning on the water with his "Papa" as he calls me.

Acknowledgements to fishing friends new and old ...

The new friends I've met during this book's creation are now the next stages of my fishing life. People like Carl Haley, whose continuous support and *forceful* coaxing, made this book a reality. I was with him when he caught his first Red-Eye, and I hope to be with him when he takes his first five pound smallmouth. He's a great guy and will have my respect and friendship from now on.

It's amazing sometimes how life works. One phone call put Darren Shell and me together. I could've found no better person to help make the pages of this book come alive than Darren. He has the passion and the know-how to help this writer say what he's feeling. I thank him for that. In him, I've found a new friend and fishing buddy who has my same passion for the smallmouth bass. I never thought that would be possible.

I must mention another good friend ... Reggie Smith, who is a good fisherman and has become one of my new fishing buddies. He's just a fun person to be around. I'm sure we're going to spend more time chasing smallmouth bass together.

One more person I have to mention is Robert Huff, or "The General" as we call him. The many conversations we've had about the things I've accomplished in my fishing life have rekindled the fire in my heart to keep on casting. Thanks, Robert.

These four people are my new friends, but I will never forget two very special friends who are no longer with me. I shared many wonderful days on the water with Porter Wagoner and Conrad Jones. I could write another whole book about the experiences with those boys … and I may someday. Gosh, I miss them.

I guess it's time to close the final pages of this book and move on. I think I might give Jay a call and see if he wants to head to the creek. I'm pretty sure he will want to. Nuthin' like a couple of grown men kicking around and splashing in the cool waters like school kids catching crawfish, Red-Eyes, and smallmouth, and loving it! We better see if Zach can come and play, too! His shoes probably haven't even dried from the last trip…

As always, I wish you safe fishing and a big catch.

Tony "The Grub and Fly Man" Bean

About the Author

Tony Bean is a smallmouth bass expert who wrote *Tony Bean's Smallmouth Guide* in 1989, and soon after became a Diawa field staff member and eventually a national team member. He helped with the design of Diawa's first smallmouth bass rod, and the rod was named after him.

He contributed to North American Fisherman's book, *Smallmouth Strategies*, and The Hunting and Fishing Library's books on smallmouth bass, *Fishing Update*, and *Secrets of the Fishing Pros*.

He was a fishing guide on Percy Priest Lake outside of Nashville, and says, "This was a great time in my life. I guided country music stars like Porter Wagoner and Jerry Reed who became a good friends and fishing buddies along with John Anderson and others."

He has also given lectures and seminars all over the country for decades. He's known as the "Grub and Fly Man."

Tony says, "I like doing the talks more than any other thing. If I had the choice between fishing for the rest of my life or doing lectures and talking with people - I would without question take the talking. I love it when people say, 'I was at the last talk you did and I caught my biggest smallmouth using one of your techniques.' That's when all of the work I've done feels worthwhile."

To learn more about Tony Bean and smallmouth bass fishing, go to www.SmallmouthSecrets.com

About the Coauthor

A historian by nature, Darren Shell has recorded local Tennessee history in a number of books from ghost stories, to lake history, to the history of the game of marbles near his native mid-south homeland of middle Tennessee. His recent emergence as a fictional author has been both playful and fun for those acquainted with his usual documentary work. His book "The Big Ones" chronicles the fish stories and interviews behind many of the biggest Smallmouth Bass ever caught in the world. He lives with his wife and daughter at his family-run marina on Dale Hollow Lake, Tennessee.

Find out more: www.DaleHollowGravedigger.com

Index

A
A Perfect Mud House, 6
Al Lindner, 35, 232
Alabama, 88, 166, 231
Amber Pepper, 74-76, 78, 80, 92, 125, 231
American Smallmouth Bass, xv, 231
Anderson, John, 227, 231
Apache Lake, 12, 77-78, 231-232
Arizona, 11-12, 48, 77-79, 99, 141, 177, 231

B
Baitfish, 6, 8, 111, 139, 148, 168, 190-191, 200, 217, 220, 231
Barometric, 9, 37, 68, 111, 116, 231
Bassmaster, 203, 231
Bassmaster Magazine, 203, 231
Bean, Uncle Grady, 7, 1-2, 21, 59-60, 66, 70, 72, 85-88, 90, 93, 137, 231
Bean, Jay, 159, 231
Bean, Jim, 7, 231
Bean, Uncle Josh, 18, 91, 136, 150, 210, 231

Bean, Zachary, 222-223, 231
Bernstein, Steve, 131, 205-206, 210, 217, 231
Blindfold Method, 25-26, 231
Bluegill, 86, 157, 160, 231
Bomber Slab Spoon, 98, 231
Bounce, 46, 138, 140, 142-143, 231
Bouncing, 11, 1, 98, 127, 139-140, 142-143, 231
Brad Weakley, 205-206, 211, 217, 233

C
Carl Haley, 52, 158-159, 219, 225, 232
Casting Patterns, 29, 231
Center Hill, 177, 231
Christian, Jack, 205, 207, 211, 217, 231
Chuck Moore, 110, 232
Connell Norton, 206, 232
Conrad Jones, 98, 103, 226, 232
Control Depth, 9, 46, 231
Corps of Engineers, 168, 231
Craig, Richard, 107, 110, 231

Crank Baits, 12, 50, 171-173, 186, 198, 206, 208, 210-211, 216, 231
Crappie, 41, 75, 94-95, 125, 231
Crawfish, 4-5, 46, 61, 64, 69-70, 73-74, 76, 92, 133-135, 137, 139, 154, 158, 160, 164-165, 181, 189, 191, 206-207, 210-217, 226, 231
Creeks, 10, 22, 59-60, 62-64, 66, 68-69, 158, 160, 166, 180, 222, 231
Critter Gitter, 98, 231
Cross-triangulation, 109, 112, 231

D

D. L. Hayes, 167, 232
Dalbuerg, Larry, 109, 231
Dale Hollow, xiii-xiv, 11, 80, 86, 94, 167-168, 177, 200, 229, 231
Dale Hollow Reservoir, 168, 231
Dan Renfro, 88, 233
Darwin, Danny, 135, 232
Della Gates, 206, 232
Diawa, 227, 232
Dodo Bird, 56
Doll Fly, 85-86, 232
Donald Paul, 115, 232
Drag, 1, 22, 55-56, 101, 232
Drop, 14, 29, 32, 40, 48, 101, 126, 128, 134, 178, 193, 195, 208, 211-212, 214, 217, 232
Dropping, 47, 178, 183, 211
Dusty Matlock, 112

E

Ewell, Jim, 144, 232

F

Fall Patterns, 189, 232
Feel, 9, 1, 10, 12-14, 19-25, 29, 38, 43-46, 48, 56, 58, 76, 101, 127, 142-143, 145, 147, 154-155, 162, 164, 172, 178, 185-186, 188, 202, 211-213, 215, 232
Finding House, 7-8, 186, 232
Fishing Library, 227, 232
Flashers, 12, 193-194
Float-N-Fly, 10, 94, 232
Float-N-Fly Smallie, 94
Fly, 10, xiii, 8, 10, 40, 78, 80, 85-88, 90-96, 100, 135-136, 150-152, 154, 186, 188, 207, 211, 214, 226-227, 232

G

Gates, Della, 206, 232
Gorman, John, 86, 232
GPS, 108-109, 232
Graphs, 12, 193-195, 197, 199
Groovy Craw, 214, 232
Grub, 9-11, 10, 19, 22-23, 29, 32-33, 39, 42-50, 69, 74-78, 80-81, 85, 90-92, 95, 100, 113, 123-129, 133-135, 139, 143, 151-152, 164, 171, 173, 181, 184-186, 189-190, 226-227, 232

H

Hair Jigs, 9, 43, 206, 232
Haley, Carl, 52, 158-159, 219, 225, 232
Harpeth River, 61, 160, 232
Harrison, Lloyd, 86, 232
Harry Renfro, 87-88, 233
Hayes, D. L., 167, 232

Houston Astros, 144, 232
Huff, Robert, 225, 232

I

In-fisherman, 35, 109, 232
Indianapolis Boat Sport and Travel Show, 88, 232
Infisherman Magazine, 35, 109, 232

J

Jack Christian, 205, 207, 211, 217, 231
Jay Bean, 159, 231
Jerry Reed, 227, 233
Jesse Walton, 11, 233
Jig, 11, 13, 18, 43, 45-46, 49-50, 78, 81, 86, 95, 113, 124, 139-140, 142-143, 160, 210, 212-213, 232
Jim Bean, 7, 231
Jim Ewell, 144, 232
John Anderson, 227, 231
John Gorman, 86, 232
Jones, Conrad, 98, 103, 226, 232

K

Kentucky Spotted Bass, 9, 232

L

Lake Apache, 12, 77-78, 231-232
Largemouth Bass, 3, 41, 74, 131, 232
Largemouth House, 9, 232
Larry Dalbuerg, 109, 231
Larry Schrader, 209-210, 217, 233
Learning *FEEL*, 9, 21-22, 46, 232

Lindner, Al, 35, 232
Lipping Technique, 219, 232
Lloyd Harrison, 86, 232
Low Barometric Pressure, 9, 37, 116

M

Maine, 88, 232
Manchester, 209, 232
Matlock, Dusty, 112
Middle Tennessee, 93, 205, 229, 232
Minnesota, 177, 232
Minnows, 5-6, 8, 12, 46, 154, 160, 232
Moore, Chuck, 110, 232
Morris Ferry Dock, 205-206, 232

N

Nashville, 20, 35, 87, 149, 168, 205, 209, 227, 232
Nolan Ryan, 135, 233
North American Fisherman, 227, 232
Norton, Connell, 206, 232
Nova Scotia, 88, 232

O

Orr, Tom, 209-210, 232

P

Paul, Donald, 115, 232
Paul Beal, 80, 231
Perch, 41, 157, 233
Percy Priest Lake, 20, 35, 42, 78, 98, 109, 136, 149, 168, 204-205, 227, 233
Pickwick Lake, 166, 233
Porter Wagoner, 141, 226-227, 233

R

Rapala, 93, 210, 233
Rapala Fat Rap, 210, 233
Rapalas, 173, 233
Rebel Deep Wee R., 210, 233
Red Eye, 160-161, 233
Red-Eye, 157-158, 161-164, 225, 233
Red-Eye Rock Bass, 161, 233
Reed, Jerry, 227, 233
Reggie Smith, 26, 225, 233
Renfro, Dan, 88, 233
Renfro, Harry, 87-88, 233
Richard Craig, 107, 110, 231
Robert Huff, 225, 232
Rock Bass, 157-159, 161, 233
Run-and-Gun, 177, 179, 182-183, 185, 233
Ryan, Nolan, 135, 233

S

Salt River, 12, 77, 233
Schrader, Larry, 209-210, 217, 233
Shad Raps, 173, 233
Shellcracker, 11, 233
Sloan, Stan, 172, 233
Smallest Tackle Box, 93, 233
Smallmouth Bass Team Club Tournament, 98, 233
Smallmouth Guide, xiii, 3, 205, 227, 233
Smallmouth Journal, 114, 233
Smallmouth Strategies, 227, 233
Smith, Reggie, 26, 225, 233
Spinner Baits, 12, 81, 120, 123-124, 169, 171-174, 210, 233
Spook, 29-32, 35, 66, 81, 93, 99, 142, 148, 152, 180, 186-187, 190-191, 220, 233
Spotted Bass, 9-10, 232-233
Squahana River, 62, 233
Stan Sloan, 172, 233
Steve Bernstein, 131, 205-206, 210, 217, 231
Sunset Marina, 86, 233
Susquanna River, 125, 233

T

Taylorsville Lake, 206, 233
Tennessee Tackle Box, 93, 233
The Big Ones, 229, 233
Tilley, Tom, 209, 217, 233
Tiny Torpedo, 190, 233
Tom Orr, 209-210, 232
Tom Tilley, 209, 217, 233

U

Uncle Grady Bean, 7, 1-2, 21, 59-60, 66, 70, 72, 85-88, 90, 93, 137, 231
Uncle Josh Bean, 18, 91, 136, 150, 210, 231

W

Walton, Jesse, 11, 233
Weakley, Brad, 205-206, 211, 217, 233
White Top Hell, 141, 233
World Record Smallmouth, 80, 86, 167, 233
Worms, 12, 59, 70, 86, 171-172, 233

Z

Zachary Bean, 222-223, 231
Zara Spook, 31, 35, 81, 93, 99, 148, 152, 186, 233